The Heart of the Prophetic

of the

Keys to flowing in a more powerful prophetic anointing.

by

Jennifer LeClaire

Unless otherwise noted, Scripture quotations are taken from the
King James Version.

The Heart of the Prophetic: Keys to flowing in a more
powerful prophetic anointing.
ISBN-10: 1-886885-24-9
ISBN-13: 978-1-886885-24-0

Published by Jennifer LeClaire Ministries
P.O. Box 3953
Hallandale Beach, Florida
33009, U.S.A.
(305) 467-4284

www.JenniferLeClaire.org

Library of Congress Control Number: 2002093363

01 02 03 04 05 06 07 ¨ 07 06 05 04 03 02 01

ENDORSEMENTS

"Jennnifer LeClaire's book, in my estimation, is one of the best books on prophecy available. Very informatively, she writes as one who believes, understands and participates in prophecy. The reader catches her intense desire to see the gift of God function powerfully in prophets of integrity. She describes about a dozen prophetic types, using illustrations, history and abundant Scriptures in a most entertaining way. This book will help anyone interested in the prophetic understand the high and holy calling -- and proper function -- of prophecy in today's church."

– Ernest Gentile
Author, *Your Sons and Daughters Shall Prophesy*

"It is so brilliant to be challenged! Every ministry needs to be aware of the kingdom standard that Jesus provokes by His presence. I loved this book! Jennifer does a bold, insightful job of discerning the precious from the worthless (Jeremiah 15:19) yet also pursues us with the love of God. Political correctness is the spirit of this age and it requires people with boldness, good character and the heart of God to stand and speak the truth with power, authority, mercy and grace. It seems that we are entering another season where prophets will be vilified, hounded and get killed again. Jennifer's book enables us to understand how important it is for us to be clean, pure and righteous so that we might die for the best of reasons ... that we are a thorn in the flesh of the church and a powerful enemy against the occult. I adored all the chapter headings; so imaginative. Now all we need is for apostles, pastors, teachers and evangelists to follow Jennifer's lead and write a book based on those titles, for their own ministry disciplines. It's great to see the prophets out in front, cleaning their own house. Good job, Jennifer!"

– Graham Cooke
Author of *Approaching the Heart of Prophecy* and *Prophecy and Responsibility*

"Everyone who wants to be prophetic or who has been exposed to prophets and prophetic ministry needs to read this book. I read this manuscript with great scrutiny for I have been a pioneer, promoter and defender of prophets and prophetic ministry for 55 years. I can honestly say that Jennifer covers some very delicate subjects with sound wisdom and integrity. The integrity of prophets is as important as the accuracy of their prophecies. People need to know that there are true and false prophets today and what makes them true or false. There are also those who are called to be prophets but who are immature, lack sound biblical knowledge, have more zeal than wisdom, or who are presumptuous. Thanks Jennifer for bringing greater clarity and correctness for prophets and saints who participate in prophetic ministry."

– Dr. Bill Hamon
Bishop, and founder of Christian International Apostolic Network
Author, *Prophets and Personal Prophecy* and several other books on the prophetic and apostolic.

"Jennifer LeClaire shares my own passion for reform in the world of prophetic ministry. I particularly appreciate her relentless emphasis on character alignment with the nature of Jesus. The Heart of the Prophetic is a solid addition to a still small - but growing - body of Christian literature seeking to root and ground prophetic ministry in the sensible soil of the eternal Word and the nature of the Lord whose word we are supposed to bring."

– R. Loren Sandford, founding pastor of New Song Fellowship, Denver, Colorado.
Author of *Purifying the Prophetic: Breaking Free from the Spirit of Self-fulfillment* and *Understanding Prophetic People: Blessings and Problems with the Prophetic Gift.*

This book is dedicated...

To every prophet in the Body of Christ who is standing in the gap, making up the hedge, manning the watchtower, sounding the alarm, equipping the saints, separating the profane from the holy, and preparing a way for the Lord.

To my precious daughter Bridgette.

I love and appreciate you all.

ACKNOWLEDGEMENTS

I give all the glory, honor and praise to Jesus Christ, to my Heavenly Father and to the Holy Ghost. I thank the Lord for giving me the grace, the faith, the strength and the perseverance to press into completing this book despite balancing family, businesses, magazine and television production, international mission trips and more. With God all things truly are possible.

CONTENTS

FOREWORD

After the resurrection of Jesus, He gave gifts to men known as apostles, prophets, evangelists, pastors and teachers, to perfect believers for the work of ministry. These are commonly referred to as five-fold ascension gifts. The resurrection of Christ marked a significant change in the order of ministry as we moved from the Old Covenant order of prophets, priests and kings to the new covenant order of five-fold ascension gifts. Before the resurrection of Christ the ministry gift of prophet was operating in the order of Aaron but after His resurrection the order changed. Now all New Testament prophets are given in the order of Melchizedek. As the order of prophetic ministry changed so did its prophetic operations.

Prophets are not scary spokespeople for God, for example, that pray down God's wrath on your soul. No longer are prophets calling down fire from heaven on surrounding armies, cursing cities and pronouncing judgment on sinners. Today New Testament prophets offer edification, exhortation and comfort. Yes, they still carry the spirit of Elijah but only in the sense of turning the hearts of people toward God, separating the holy from the profane and encouraging a more intimate relationship with Christ.

New Testament prophets continue to pray, stand in the gap, make up the hedge, battle principalities and powers and demonic activity. Yet one thing is certain, true prophets are not merchandisers or shamans. Nor do they seek to prophesy using occult methods such as Kabbalah. They don't need esoteric methods to help them prophesy or find hidden wisdom in letters, numbers or symbols.

True prophetic ministry comes by the Holy Spirit alone. The testimony of Jesus, our Christ, is the spirit of prophecy (Revelation 19:10). Prophetic ministry will always point to Jesus, His perfect character, His tender heart, His mercy and His righteous way of doing things. Jesus is the way, the truth and the life. He came that we might have life more abundantly.

This book is about the heart of the prophet, the

depository of God's prophetic spirit. Jennifer dares to address the hijacking of prophetic ministry in some circles by the spirit of Jezebel, divination and spiritual mystics. She is pointed, direct and hammers them hard but with a right spirit. She defends true prophetic ministry and understands the importance of right motives and desires to put Christ first. My prayer is that the Holy Spirit will lead you and guide you in truth as you read this powerful book. I believe if you read this essay with a humble heart it will help you become a better prophetic minister.

The Lord spoke to me concerning prophetic ministry and specifically the prophets. He said, "My prophets will begin to relate to me in a different way." I think The Heart of the Prophetic will help that happen. Prophets and prophetic ministry are signs of a healthy church. Check your motives, put Jesus first in everything and allow your gift to equip others to do what God has called them to do, make a difference with their lives and bring glory to Christ.

Jonas Clark
Founder of Spirit of Life Ministries

PREFACE

If you read my columns on prophetic ministry in major international Christian magazines, then you've discerned that I'm just plain passionate about the prophetic ministry. Prophets are vital to the Body of Christ.

Over the years in my capacity of editor of *The Voice* I have had the opportunity to mingle with many leaders in prophetic ministry for whom I have the utmost respect. However, I've also seen disturbing goings on in prophetic ministry that have stirred my spirit to pen articles regarding character issues and spirits that muck up the prophetic river. As God began to aggressively restore prophetic ministry in the 1980s it seems wolves in sheep's clothing got a head start on true prophetic gifts the Lord has given the Church (Ephesians 4:11).

While disclosing the false, I have also sought to edify true prophets who are stowed away in caves by the forces of religion and to comfort prophets who seem stuck in desert places with a bold word of the Lord that few will accept. I strongly believe for each visible prophet who is misrepresenting the prophetic ministry there are thousands of others who are functioning in the unadulterated ministry of prophet without the glam and glory. We may not know their names, but they are making an impact for Jesus. Thank God for them.

Finally, my essays often seek to exhort prophets and intercessors to look deep within their own souls for worldly fragments that skew their perspective of themselves, their brothers and sisters in Christ, and the Lord Himself. The seasoned British prophet Graham Cooke once said that a person could only prophesy in line with their revelation of who Jesus is. If our perception of Jesus is inaccurate, incomplete or immature, then our prophetic utterances will reflect as much. If our revelation of Jesus is as a judgmental God waiting to whack us upside the head at the mere hint of a mistake, then our prophecies will be filtered through this fear. Just as any believer, prophets and intercessors must know who they are in Christ and who Christ is in them. But prophets and intercessors must also be willing to look at those areas of their lives that are anything but Christ-like and crucify character flaws daily while resisting the spirits that try to creep in to pervert. The more accurate our perception of Jesus and the more Christ-like we are, the more accurate our prophetic utterances will be.

Although there are many wonderful books on how to hear from God – and we need every one of them so that the saints can get equipped to know the voice and will of God for themselves – there are far too few materials that offer keys to flowing more accurately. What's more, there is far too little talk in the Body of Christ about the character of Christ, or even the character of the prophets who foretold His coming. Elijah wasn't perfect. He entertained Jezebel's fearful threats. But he also received the Lord's correction and completed his ministry with integrity. Isaiah didn't come to the Lord with a perfect heart. He confessed the sinfulness of his mouth and withstood the fire of the Lord to cleanse him from unrighteousness. As New Testament prophets and intercessors, the Lord does not demand perfection. But he does demand a pliable heart that is as sensitive to His correction as it is to His unction to prophesy at the main event.

My goal with this book is to help prophets and

intercessors speak forth what says the Lord with greater boldness – boldness that has its roots in confidence that we are hearing accurately; boldness that comes from a conviction that the Lord's will must be communicated to the Church in these last days; and boldness with a clean heart that will not compromise God's voice even in the face of the greatest temptation.

Listen, we must not allow the extremes, errors and excesses to scare us away from prophets or prophetic ministry. Likewise, we must not tolerate the underlying issues that lead to these extremes, errors and excesses. And we must not be ignorant to snares of the devil that pervert the voice of God and hijack prophetic ministry. There is enormous opposition to prophetic ministry and plenty of potholes on the supernatural highway to your destiny. Indeed, the spirits of Jezebel and Baal have already infiltrated some segments of prophetic ministry and false prophetic cults have risen with a vengeance. Their utterances begin with "thus saith the Lord" but the curses and judgments are by no means coming from His Spirit. This must not be so. God needs prophets and intercessors who are willing to count the cost, purify their hearts and take a stand for Him.

In their classic book, "The Elijah Task: A Call to Prophets and Intercessors,"[1] John and Paula Sandford discuss much-needed topics such as the restoration of prophetic ministry, the call of the prophet, the discipline and training of a prophet, and the proper discharge of the prophet's duty. The prophetic duo makes clear in their text that prophets and intercessors must let the Holy Spirit shine light into the deepest recesses of their hearts:

"When God shows a prophet some hidden forgotten sin, it is to save him from the effects of that sin. We, however, usually object violently and try to suppress the sight. We hate to look at our sin because we think it disqualifies us (which only shows how much we are still relying on ourselves and not in Christ). 'All things that are reproved are made manifest by the light: for whatsoever doth make manifest is light' (Ephesians 5:13). We should be glad to see our sin, for that will mean healing, but 'men loved darkness rather than light because their deeds were evil'" (John 3:19)."

Let us be willing to allow the Holy Spirit entrance into every corner of our souls to reveal sinful attitudes, tendencies and character flaws that could open the door to the enemy. Let us not take a haughty position and say we have no sin, lest we be deceived before we ever get started. Let us have the same mind that was in Christ Jesus, who humbled Himself (Philippians 2:5) and let us learn obedience from the things we suffer (Hebrews

5:8). I assure you the sufferings of this present time are not worthy to be compared with the glory that is to be revealed in us (Romans 8:18).

This book may infuriate some, but that is not my intention. It's inevitable that the truth will anger some, but it will also set many others free to be all that God has called them to be. It will protect them from the little foxes. In the wake of dam disasters that have killed precious lives and flooded cities, engineers often discovered a small leak in the concrete that, if repaired, could have averted tragedy. My goal is to help you discover those little leaks so the Holy Ghost can help you plug them.

God has a purpose for prophetic ministry and He needs His prophets willing to walk worthy of the vocation (Ephesians 4:1). Will you accept the challenge to come to new levels of accuracy in the prophetic? With it comes a dare to examine yourself, empty yourself, and fill yourself with the Spirit of God. Like John the Baptist, we must decrease that Jesus might increase (John 3:30). I pray what I have written on the pages that make up this book will serve as a prophetic wake up call to all of us and, in some small way, contribute to the complete restoration of vital prophetic ministry in purity and humility. He that has ears let him hear (Matthew 11:15).

Chapter 1

CALLING
ALL PROPHETS

*And he gave some, apostles; and some, prophets; and some, evangelists; and some, pastors and teachers; For the perfecting of the saints, for the work of the ministry, for the edifying of the body of Christ: Till we all come in the unity of the faith, and of the knowledge of the Son of God, unto a perfect man, unto the measure of the stature of the fulness of Christ....
(Ephesians 4:11-13)*

The Church has not always been kind to its prophets. In fact, prophets have a history of getting beaten, imprisoned, and even sawed in half by those who called themselves godly. But I believe the prophet's hour has come and the Church will appreciate this gift more in the days ahead. Indeed, if there was ever a time in the history of the Church when we needed holy, stable, bold, uncompromising prophets it's right now. There are wars and rumors of wars, failing economies, starving children, ungodly governments, and Islamic extremists rising up to take dominion…and that's just in the world.

The Church of Jesus Christ has challenges within itself. Tares are hidden among the wheat, false teachers and prophets are seducing the sheep, immorality is mowing down high-profile leaders, and apathy is threatening to overcome passion. Bona fide prophets are part and parcel of the solution. The other parts and parcels are apostles, pastors, teachers and evangelists (Ephesians 4:11).

Where would the Body of Christ be without prophets? It would be incomplete with no hope of ever fully maturing. Jesus gave equipping gifts to His Church to help Christians grow up and unify to build a holy temple where the Spirit of God feels at home. Removing even one of those five factors (graces) out of the spiritual equation results in an erroneous solution to the challenges facing the Church.

Indeed, we need all five spiritual "tools" to build a glorious Church without spot or wrinkle. The Church that the gates of hell shall not prevail against is one built on the foundation of apostles and prophets, Jesus Christ Himself being the chief cornerstone (Ephesians 2:20). Keep in mind that the cornerstone is the stone in the foundation that rests at the outer corner of two intersecting walls. It is the stone to which all others in the foundation must be aligned. If apostles and prophets are not aligned to the chief cornerstone, then the foundation will have gaps. Think of it this way: Termites can enter a building through foundational gaps that are as small as 1/32 inch. So can toxic vapors that reduce the indoor air quality and cause inhabitants to get sick. Apostles and prophets, then, must be aligned to Jesus so that spiritual termites (read: heresies, disunity, and other destructive forces) are not allowed to infiltrate the Church and eat away at its structure. True apostles, prophets and intercessors are willing to make adjustments.

Make no mistake, the Church's destiny is guaranteed to be glorious without spot or wrinkle and prophets play a key role. I believe prophets will be at the forefront of a fourth Great Awakening that will happen in my lifetime. The Lord has spoken to me, as well as many others, about this Great Awakening. God is calling all prophets to report for duty with eyes wide open to help prepare the way for this great outpouring.

DESTINY OR DECEPTION? YOU DECIDE.

As you look around, you will surely notice that times are changing in the Body of Christ. God is raising up companies of prophets and congregations of prophetic people to make the paths straight for His purposes in these last days. Today, the Apostolic Movement (the restoration of apostles to the Church) is building a platform to make room for modern-day prophets to take their proper position in the Body of Christ. Beyond serving as watchmen, sounding the alarm and interceding, New Testament prophets are called to equip the saints to build the Church so the equipped saints can change the world for Jesus Christ. We need the entire army working together in unison to enforce the fullness of Kingdom rule on earth as it is in heaven. We need the prophets.

Of course, the devil knows his time is limited. Satan sees the plan of God unfolding right before his evil eyes. He knows with the restoration of apostles and prophets God's plan has accelerated, and he will stop at absolutely nothing to derail true prophetic ministry. If the devil can pervert the prophetic – the very voice of God – then the Church will not walk in the fullness of Christ. Souls will die and go to hell that could otherwise be reached with the truth of the Gospel of the Kingdom. And the devil can extend his influence in the earth a little while longer.

It should be noted that this is not the first time in Church history God has tried to restore the ministries of apostles and prophets. Unfortunately, the spirit of religion has foiled this restoration in times past. (The Latter Rain Movement is a prime example.) However, I believe the hour has come. This time, the question is not whether the apostolic and prophetic movements will stand in the face of religious persecution. The question is whether or not His prophets will stand and withstand the enemy's attempts to woo them to the road of deception, or just quit the race altogether.

The devil can't sideline prophets and intercessors. Ultimately, we have to sideline ourselves.

PAY NOW OR PAY LATER

Doubtless, Satan comes to steal, kill and destroy the prophetic ministry. But he can only do that if he finds something in the prophet to work with. What is the devil looking for? Largely, character flaws. Areas of our lives that aren't submitted to the Word of God. Places in our hearts still shrouded in darkness. Nooks and crannies in our souls clouded with selfish ambition. Allegiances with the ways of the world.

> "For all that is in the world, the lust of the flesh, and the lust of the eyes, and the pride of life, is not of the Father, but is of the world" (1 John 2:16).

Listen, prophets...Don't gloss over this because you've heard it before.

The devil doesn't have any new tricks. He doesn't need any new ones. The old ones seem to work just fine. This is why God takes prophets through a making process. I see far too many prophets who forego this making in a hurry to reach the circuits. The outcome is often devastating.

Here's the bottom line: We can pay now or we can pay later. It's our choice. You can pay the price now to deal with attitudes and roots in your life that are anything but Christ-like. (That price is often self-denial rather than self-indulgence.) Or you can decide to run the race carrying the cumbersome weights of sin and self as you chase ministry opportunities that seem too good to pass up. The cost of taking the time to prepare yourself for the higher calling may seem too much to bear. Impatience clouds the realities of readiness. But I guarantee this: If you put off reconciling your character debts today you'll pay the piper with compounded interest later. We must follow His leading so that our gifts don't take us where our character won't keep us. There's no time to waste. God has accelerated the preparation process, it seems. Yield to that preparation rather than resisting or even neglecting to understand that time is short.

That last statement reminds me of a story British TV personality Michael Aspel once related about Sir John Gielgud. Gielgud is an actor known for his Shakespearean roles. In her book "100 Best After-Dinner Stories,"[2] Phyllis Schindler records Aspel's recollections of rehearsals for Shakespeare's Oedipus at the National Theater. Apparently, rehearsals weren't going well and the director, Peter Hall, called the cast together to tell them as much. His complaint: The actors weren't displaying enough fire and passion. His remedy: Come up on stage, one at a time, and say something that would terrify him. "Each member of the cast stepped forward and roared obscenities and threats into the darkness," Aspel tells. "Finally, Sir John [Gielgud] sauntered to the front of the stage, took a languid draw from his cigarette and said: 'We open in two weeks!'"

If unsaved and carnal people can muster that kind of passion, how much more God's holy prophets? When I think of that from a spiritual perspective, it puts the fear of the Lord in me. God is waiting to draw the curtains for the opening of the great scene that ushers in the second coming of our Messiah. Unlike a Shakespearean play that could very well open with unprepared actors, God's play won't open with an unprepared Church. Prophets are called to make a highway for Jesus – to prepare a people for Him. I shudder to think of wasting His time by refusing to yield to the Potter's Hand, don't you? We've got to get ready and get others ready to do what they are called to do. There is no time to waste.

PURIFYING THE PROPHETIC

It's possible to rise in spiritual ranking despite your hidden character flaws, but you won't be able to maintain your position if you don't minister God's way. The Bible says if the Lord isn't building the house we are laboring in vain (Psalm 127:1). Well, the Lord isn't going to build a prophetic lighthouse to the nations on a foundation with character cracks.

If you want to prophesy over nations, if you want to impact the lives of the masses, if you want to be a general in the great company of prophets and intercessors the Lord is raising, then you need to fill up the cracks in your character with the fruit of the Spirit. You need to purify your prophetic flow now because the Bible says what we do in secret will be shouted from the rooftops. In other words, your sin will find you out. It's just a matter of time.

The devil is strategic. He waits until you can influence tens of thousands of people and then shows the trump card – that hidden character flaw that you never wanted to deal with – and pulls the rug out from under your ministry and all those who trusted in it. Over the years we've seen scandals disgrace prophets and leave hurting people to pick up the pieces. I continue to watch believers who fall prey to merchandising prophets who leave them with empty pockets and empty promises. I've seen behind the curtain and it's anything but God's will for the prophetic. This is a vital ministry and we must take the responsibility to purify ourselves so the devil can find nothing in us.

LOOK IN THE MIRROR

When the prince of this world came to Jesus with his various temptations he found nothing in Him (John 14:30). There was no hidden sin in His life. And there were no hidden character issues that He refused to deal with. The highway to prophetic destiny was free and clear. He avoided every enticement the devil offered. Are you able to say the same?

I've heard some say that character issues don't matter in the prophetic. Such statements floor me. As you read this book, I beseech you by the mercies of

God to examine your heart. Whether you are called as a prophet or are looking to develop the prophetic grace that is available to every believer through the baptism of the Holy Ghost, there are potholes strategically positioned on the spiritual highway on which you are traveling. If you work with the Holy Spirit to work out the character of Jesus in you, you will remain sensitive to His leading and steer clear of the enemy's plan to leave you stranded on the side of the road. Jesus, the Prophet, is the Way, the Truth and the Life. In Him there is no darkness, no stumbling – and no potholes.

The Lord doesn't expect us to be perfect, but He does expect us to be willing to look at ourselves in the mirror of the Word and allow the Holy Spirit to convict us of sin so the blood of Jesus can cleanse us from all unrighteousness. That requires humility of heart and a willingness to lay aside childish things and walk worthy of the prophetic vocation.

PROPHETIC PROTOCOLS

Prophets are spiritually equipped to serve as the eyes, ears and voice to the Body of Christ. That eye must be single toward the purposes and plans of God, unpolluted by the ways of the world. Before we move on to identify some of the spirits attacking the prophetic ministry and the character flaws that open the door to their influence, I want to leave you with a Scripture to meditate. It will help prepare and guard your heart for what God has called you to. I especially like the way 2 Peter 1:3-10 reads in the Amplified Bible.

> (3) "For His divine power has bestowed upon us all things that [are requisite and suited] to life and godliness, through the [full, personal] knowledge of Him Who called us by and to His own glory and excellence (virtue)."

> (4) "By means of these He has bestowed on us His precious and exceedingly great promises, so that through them you may escape [by flight] from the moral decay (rottenness and corruption) that is in the world because of covetousness (lust and greed), and become sharers (partakers) of the divine nature."

In Verses three and four of this passage, we see that God has already given us everything we need to succeed. He has called us to be holy even as He is holy.

Through this promise, we can resist the temptations of the lust of the eyes, the lust of the flesh and the pride of life and share in His character. But we have a part to play…Let's read on.

(5) "For this very reason, adding your diligence [to the divine promises], employ every effort in exercising your faith to develop virtue (excellence, resolution, Christian energy), and in [exercising] virtue [develop] knowledge (intelligence),"

(6) "And in [exercising] knowledge [develop] self-control, and in [exercising] self-control [develop] steadfastness (patience, endurance), and in [exercising] steadfastness [develop] godliness (piety),

(7) "And in [exercising] godliness [develop] brotherly affection, and in [exercising] brotherly affection [develop] Christian love."

In Verses five through seven, we learn that our role is to be diligent to exercise our faith. We are called to work out these characteristics that God has deposited in our spirits so good fruit might be manifest in our lives. The world and the Church will judge us by our fruit. If they see these qualities in our character, our prophetic voice will carry the credibility necessary to bring lasting change. If they see the works of the flesh Paul outlines in Galatians, we will bring a reproach on the prophetic ministry. Let's read on...

(8) "For as these qualities are yours and increasingly abound in you, they will keep [you] from being idle or unfruitful unto the [full personal] knowledge of our Lord Jesus Christ (the Messiah, the Anointed One)."

(9) "For whoever lacks these qualities is blind, [spiritually] shortsighted, seeing only what is near to him, and has become oblivious [to the fact] that he was cleansed from his old sins.

(10) "Because of this, brethren, be all the more solicitous and eager to make sure (to ratify, to strengthen, to make steadfast) your calling and election; for if you do this, you will never stumble or fall."

In Verses eight, nine and 10, the Holy Ghost shows us contrasting pictures that drive the point home. Whoever lacks these qualities is blind and spiritually shortsighted. Now tell me, what good is a prophet who is blind or even spiritually shortsighted? Selah. Pause and think about that for a moment. If you want to make your calling and election devil-proof, follow Peter's Holy Spirit-inspired advice. If you do, the Bible promises that you won't fall. As a matter of fact, you won't even stumble. What an awesome promise!

A DOUBLE-PORTION ANOINTING

Again, whether you are a prophet or a prophetic believer, God needs you in this hour. You are vital to His plan. This book is written in the spirit of humility and with plenty of self-examination that I encourage you to undergo. Sure, I could offer you lots of exciting, hyped up Christianese about the power of the prophetic and how you can walk in signs, wonders and miracles. I could tell you character doesn't matter; that the gift of God within you is all you need. But if I told you that I'd be robbing you of an opportunity to walk in the greater grace. I'd also have to answer to God for selling you a book full of baloney. Character matters.

Just as Elisha performed twice as many miracles as his spiritual father Elijah, I believe there is coming to the Body of Christ a great outpouring, a double portion of the prophetic anointing for the last days. But if you want to carry the spirit God is pouring out upon His prophets, you'll have to empty yourself of everything that doesn't line up with the character of the Prophet, Jesus Christ.

Are you ready to prepare yourself to be all God created you to be? Journey with me as we reveal the heart of the prophetic ministry, some of your spiritual enemies and how you can guard yourself from them so that you can flow more accurately and make your mark on this world for the Maker.

PROPHETIC KEYS

+ The devil is looking to derail us with character flaws: areas of our lives that aren't submitted to the Word of God, places in our hearts still shrouded in darkness, nooks and crannies in our souls clouded with deception, allegiances with the ways of the world.

◆   Impatience clouds the realities of readiness.

◆   If you want to prophesy over nations, if you want to impact the lives of the masses, if you want to be a general in the great company of prophets and intercessors the Lord is raising up, then you need to fill up the potholes in your character with the fruit of the Spirit.

◆   If you want to carry the spirit God is pouring out upon His prophets, you'll have to empty yourself of everything that doesn't line up with the character of the Prophet, Jesus Christ.

◆   If you work with the Holy Spirit to work out the character of Jesus in you, you will remain sensitive to His leading and steer clear of the enemy's plan to leave you stranded on the side of the road.

.

Chapter 2

THE HEART
OF THE PROPHETIC

*Now if perfection (a perfect fellowship between God and the
worshiper) had been attainable by the Levitical priesthood
– for under it the people were given the Law – why was it
further necessary that there should arise another and different
kind of Priest, one after the order of Melchizedek, rather
than one appointed after the order and rank of Aaron? For
when there is a change in the priesthood, there is of necessity
an alteration of the law [concerning the priesthood] as well
(Hebrews 7:11-12 AMP)*

One and a half million Americans will have a heart
attack next year, according to American Heart

Association (AHA) estimates. About 500,000 of those heart attack victims will die. Let's look at it through a different prism: A heart attack occurs about every 20 seconds and someone dies from a heart attack about every minute. Heart failure is on the rise.

Now put on your spiritual glasses and follow me for a minute. I'm going somewhere with this.

A heart attack occurs when the blood supply to part of the heart muscle is severely reduced or stopped, the AHA explains. The reduction or stoppage happens when one or more of the coronary arteries supplying blood to the heart muscle is blocked. This is usually caused by the buildup of what's called plaque (deposits of fat-like substances). The plaque can eventually burst, tear or rupture, creating a "snag" where a blood clot forms and blocks the artery. This leads to a heart attack.

What does this have to do with the prophetic ministry? Everything. The heart of the prophetic – and the motive of the prophet – is under attack on a grand scale. It's under attack by polished showmen with plenty of hype and little anointing who think the prophetic gift is for merchandising or controlling people. It's under attack by spirits of religion that use the prophetic as a vehicle for prominence and position. It's under attack by Jezebel spirits that use fearful prophecies of cursing and judgment to gain power. It's even under attack by our own pride that thinks it's all about us. The heart of the prophetic is a target and the aim of the attack is to keep the prophetic ministry in you from functioning properly and in doing so cause great damage to the Body.

In a spiritual parallel to the natural example of a heart attack the AHA offers, think of the blood supply as the anointing of God. If the anointing of God is severely reduced or stopped because our souls are blocked with a buildup of plaque (deposits of sin and self) then we'll eventually run into a snag that will hinder our effectiveness in ministry. Just as doctors encourage us to stay away from fried, fatty foods that are high in cholesterol because it clogs the arteries, the Great Physician encourages us to shun all forms of sin because it blocks the flow of anointing over our lives. So I maintain that we need the prophets, but as you can see we need prophets without clogged spiritual arteries.

BUSTING PROPHETIC MYTHS

The restoration of prophetic ministry has come a long way. With it came an interesting phenomenon. It almost seems as if everybody wants to be a prophet. But I wonder...If people truly understood what it meant to stand in the office of a prophet, would they really want to do the work of a prophet? There are some myths about prophetic ministry I intend to bust right now. First, the New Testament prophet's primary function is not to stand under a celebrity spotlight in the midst of the minstrel's melodies and announce what says the Spirit of God. The New Testament prophet is not called to pronounce judgments and curses on cities, nations and people. In short, the New Testament prophet is not called to function in all the same ways as Old Testament prophets. After all, we have a better covenant based on better promises. God didn't change but His covenant did – and so did His purpose for His prophets. Old Testament prophets primarily foretold the Messiah's coming and warned the Israelites about the ultimate consequences of following other gods. In the New Testament, the primary purpose of the prophet is found in the Book of Ephesians:

"And he gave some, apostles; and some, prophets; and some, evangelists; and some, pastors and teachers; For the perfecting of the saints, for the work of the ministry, for the edifying of the body of Christ: Till we all come in the unity of the faith, and of the knowledge of the Son of God, unto a perfect man, unto the measure of the stature of the fulness of Christ..." (Ephesians 4:11-13)

Of course, that is not to say that New Testament prophets will not prophesy over a congregation or in a prayer line as the minstrels help to usher in the spirit of prophesy. It doesn't mean that New Testament prophets won't deliver true correction of the Spirit, either. What we have to keep in mind when we look at the heart of the prophetic in New Testament times is the covenant. Jesus Christ is the Prophet and He is our prototype. As a New Testament prophet, His primary function was to equip people for works of service in the Kingdom of God. Jesus taught His disciples. He prepared them for the ministry they would inherit after He ascended to the right hand of the Father.

Now that we have that out of the way, it is clear that New Testament and Old Testament prophets do share some common functions. In those common functions, I believe, you will find the heart of the prophetic.

STANDING IN THE GAP

Let's talk a little bit about the priesthood of the prophetic. The Bible says we are priests and kings (1

Peter 2:9). What is the priesthood of the prophetic? Well, a priest in the common sense of the word is one who is authorized to act as an intermediary between man and God. We know that Jesus is our mediator. Nevertheless, God has chosen not to do anything in the earth unless someone in this realm makes a petition. In other words, God won't work unless we pray. The Lord said,

> "I sought for a man among them, that should make up the hedge, and stand in the gap before me for the land, that I should not destroy it: but found none" (Ezekiel 22:30).

Let those words not escape the Lord's lips in this generation!

The truth is, every believer is called to intercede. The Bible says, "If My people who are called by my name, shall humble themselves, and pray, and seek my face, and turn from their wicked ways; then will I hear from heaven, and will forgive their sin, and heal their land" (2 Chronicles 7:14). If you are among His people, you are called to pray. And in 1 Timothy 2:1, the Apostle Paul exhorts us to offer supplications, prayers, intercessions and giving thanks for all men. Jesus ever lives to make intercession for us, but that does not do away with our responsibility to pray. Still, there are those with calls to serve as intercessors and prophets. You've probably heard it said that every prophet is an intercessor, but not every intercessor is a prophet. Thank God for all those who are doers of 1 Timothy 2:1 and 2 Chronicles 7:14.

With these truths established, we must move deeper into the heart of the prophetic priestly duty to make intercession. The very first time you see the word "prophet" in the Bible, it is connected to prayer. In the Book of Genesis when Abimelech took Abraham's wife in innocence, the Lord said, "Now return the man's wife, for he is a prophet, and he will pray for you and you will live..." (Genesis 20:7). Old Testament or New, you can't separate the prophet from prayer. It is the lifeblood of the prophetic because it is our connection with God and His will.

Surely the Lord God does nothing, but that He revealeth His secrets to His servants the prophets (Amos 3:7). Indeed, but the secret of the Lord is with those that fear Him; He will shew them His covenant (Psalm 25:14). How can we expect to hear accurately? How can we expect to deliver a powerful, life-changing, nation-shaking prophetic utterance? How can we expect to function in the office of the prophet if we take intercession out of the mix? Failing to pray and intercede, friends, demonstrates a lack of the fear of the Lord because His word clearly commands it. His secrets are with those who fear Him. How can you stand in the gap if you are self-willed, self-centered and judgmental? Selah. Ask the Lord to cover you with a spirit of prayer that you would not grow weary of standing in the gap, no matter how vast it may be.

THE HEART-TURNING MINISTRY

Another function of prophetic ministry shared by prophets operating under both the old and new covenants is turning the hearts of the fathers toward the sons and the hearts of the sons toward the fathers. The Prophet Malachi proclaimed the word of the Lord in the fourth chapter of his prophetic chronicles:

> "Behold, I will send you Elijah the prophet before the coming of the great and dreadful day of the Lord: And he shall turn the heart of the fathers to the children, and the heart of the children to their fathers, lest I come and smite the earth with a curse" (Malachi 4:5-6).

This is a telling Verse of Scripture. The Amplified version calls this turning a "reconciliation produced by repentance of the ungodly." This speaks of an evangelistic thrust. But it also speaks of calls for repentance of God's children in the Church who are walking in rebellion. Born again believers are holy and without blame before Him in love, but we all know the behavior of born again believers is not always godly.

Yet there is another angle from which we can view Malachi's mandate. If prophecy reveals the heart of God, then the prophetic ministry is called to turn the hearts of His children toward the matters of His heart. In other words, it is not enough to breeze through a congregation with a prophetic utterance on your way to the next meeting. Too many times prophetic words are delivered, but not prayed through. I believe this is because the hearts of the children were not completely turned toward the heart of the Father in the matter. The prophetic word evoked a shout and a few goose bumps, but soon found its way into a drawer, waiting half-heartedly for God to bring it to pass.

Prophets have a responsibility not just to declare the heart of God but also to work with Him to turn the hearts of the people toward His heart in any matter He chooses to share. Teaching saints what they must do to receive the promise in the prophetic word by tapping into the Scriptures is one way to help ensure the heart of the people are turned to the heart of the Father. Teaching them how to maintain or respond to what the Lord says He has given them in a prophetic word is another. Teaching them to pray the word through is yet another. And teaching them to wage a good warfare with the prophetic word is still another.

How can you turn the hearts of men to the Father if your own heart is not fully turned toward Him? Ask the Lord to show you any area of your life where your heart – your will – is not submitted to Him. It could be that your heart is not turned toward Him in the area of finances or submission to authority. It could be that your heart is not turned toward Him in the area of walking in love with the unlovely. It could be that your heart is not turned toward Him in the area of patiently waiting for His will in your life. It's important to line your heart up with God's heart because I don't believe you can turn the hearts of the children toward the Father in areas where your heart is not congruent with the Master. You will rather compromise and lead them astray in those areas rather than calling for repentance, which is required in the heart-turning process.

THE REFORMING SPIRIT

Old Testament or New, the spirit of reformation charges prophetic ministry. The prophetic ministry is called to bring change – positive change. This reforming spirit brings hope to people. Elijah is a prime example. He challenged the people to declare whom they would serve: Jehovah or Baal. His reformation message sought to turn the hearts of men away from pagan gods. What about the Prophet Haggai? Haggai's reforming message challenged Israel to rebuild God's temple so they could receive His blessings. Don't forget the Prophetess Deborah. She united the Israelites against the Canaanites during a time no men were willing to lead. She led her nation in victory, bringing freedom to Israel.

The Old Testament is filled with prophetic reformers. Ezekiel, Jeremiah, Isaiah, Malachi. It's a common characteristic that accompanies the prophetic anointing in any era. Moving into the New Testament, we see John the Baptist with his reformation message and, of course, Jesus, the mighty Reformer, who came to reform religion as His day knew it. You can't divide a reformation mindset from the prophetic. Prophets have reformation in their DNA. Their goal is to see God's best for people and nations and they take action to bring change, whether that is in the heart of man, in spiritual warfare, or in building efforts of some sort. The apostles, remember, aren't the only five-fold ascension gift called to build. The prophetic ministry builds and plants. The apostle and prophet build in different ways, but their desire is the same: to see the glorious Church without spot or wrinkle filled with equipped, triumphant saints.

PREPARING A PEOPLE FOR THE LORD

The heart of the prophetic is in preparation. Prophets are called to prepare a way for the Lord and to prepare people for the Lord. John the Baptist, a transitional prophet being the last of Old Testament prophets and the first of New Testament prophets, was called to prepare a way for the Lord, to make His paths straight (Matthew 3:2-4). He was a messenger and this was his message: "Repent!"

John the Baptist carried the spirit of Elijah that Malachi discussed. The Bible says John was filled with the Holy Ghost, even from his mother's womb (Luke 1:15). An angel of the Lord told Zacharias, John's father, what to expect before the child was conceived:

"And he will [himself] go before Him in the spirit and power of Elijah, to turn back the hearts of the fathers to the children, and the disobedient and incredulous and unpersuadable to the wisdom of the upright [which is the knowledge and holy love of the will of God] – in order to make ready for the Lord a people [perfectly] prepared [in spirit, adjusted and disposed and placed in the right moral state]"(Luke 1:17 AMP).

So we see the angel of the Lord prophesied that John would come in the spirit and power of Elijah to turn the hearts of the fathers toward the children and the hearts of the children back to the will of God. Preparing a people for the Lord, then, is preparing their spirit and their souls, their spirits to receive wisdom and revelation in the knowledge of Him and their souls to submit to the Spirit.

How can you prepare a people for the Lord when your own heart is not prepared? Remember, John the Baptist was prepared in the wilderness. John the Baptist was a voice crying in the wilderness for many years before he made his public debut. Prophets must go through a period of wilderness preparation in order to be effective for the Lord. The making process is a subject for another book, but suffice it to say that the prophet must first be prepared before he can prepare a people for the Lord. Yes, there are stages and levels of preparation and I believe the Lord will use us where we are to do what He can trust us to do. And, yes, I believe that the times have accelerated.

Just as scientists have proven that the world is spinning faster on its axis, I believe God is also speeding up the preparation process, as I mentioned earlier. Our job is to submit to it. You submit to it by being sensitive to the Spirit and quick to repent. If the Holy Ghost is dealing with you about something, why not just cooperate with Him and get it over quickly? Yes, it's painful, but it's more painful in the end not to go through that fire. You can feel the pain of preparation today or the pain of regret tomorrow.

SEPARATING THE HOLY FROM THE PROFANE

The heart of the prophetic ministry also includes separating the holy from the profane. Unfortunately, too many prophets shut their eyes to profanity, or worse yet engage in it, rather than bringing a spiritual winnowing fork to separate the wheat from the tares, the holy from the profane.

The Lord tells us to be holy even as He is holy (1 Peter 1:16). To be holy is to be devoted entirely to God and His work, to be consecrated for His purposes. The word "profane" simply means unsanctified, secular, or irreverent. It doesn't take a prophet to discern the difference, yet it does take a prophetic anointing to separate the holy from the profane when the two have grown up together. This is part of the prophetic anointing to root out (Jeremiah 1) and may require deliverance ministry.

But that's just one way to separate the holy from the profane. The second way prevents demonic strongholds in the first place by calling a sin a sin before the devil takes up residence in the believer's soul. Prophets carry a grace that convicts people of their sin. We know that Jonah went to Nineveh with a message of repentance. The people believed God, proclaimed a fast, and put on sackcloth, from the greatest of them even to the least of them (Jonah 3). We know that the Lord told Isaiah to "cry aloud, lift up thy voice like a trumpet, and shew my people their transgression..." (Isaiah 58:1). And we know that the Lord told Ezekiel to "cause Jerusalem to know her abominations" (Ezekiel 16:1-2).

This is an area where Old Testament and New Testament operations intersect, for the Apostle Paul wrote in his first epistle to the church at Corinth about the grace of the prophetic to convict of sin:

"But if all prophesy [giving inspired testimony and interpreting the divine will and purpose] and an unbeliever or untaught outsider comes in, he is told of his sin and reproved and convicted and convinced by all, and his defects and needs are examined (estimated, determined) and he is called to account by all, The secrets of his heart are laid bare; and so, falling on [his] face, he will worship God, declaring that God is among you in very truth" (1 Corinthians 14:24-25 AMP).

Now here's the deal. It's not only unbelievers who need to be encouraged to separate the profane from the holy. Christians, too, can backslide into secular living. The Apostle James warned believers that friendship with the world is enmity with God. Enmity describes a mutual ill will. Therefore, whoever wishes to be a friend of the world makes himself an enemy with God (James 4:4). In other words, we can't live like the world lives. That doesn't mean that you should alienate yourself from the world. How can we reach the world if we avoid the world?

I believe being in the world but not of the world means that when we do have to mingle with the world, we go in prayed up. We don't enjoy the works of wickedness in the marketplace or take part in them. Instead, we model the way of holiness without being holier than thou. When we go home, we pray again for those who are entangled in the deep recesses of a sinful world. We make intercession for them. Now, in the Church, we need to take another approach. Prophets need to speak the truth in love so that the saints can grow up (Ephesians 4:15). That love-inspired truth is the agent that will separate the holy from the profane.

How can you separate the holy from the profane if your own heart is impure? If you have sin in a certain area of your life, how can you boldly speak against it without falling into yet another sin – hypocrisy? We've seen this happen again and again in the Church, haven't we? Some of the staunchest advocates against abominations have been found to be partakers of the selfsame sin. That brings a reproach on the name of Jesus and pain to those who trusted them.

Like I said before, the devil will show his trump card at just the right time. People may get away with unscrupulous acts for a season, but God is not mocked.

The sin will be found out. Why not confess it and receive cleansing rather than waiting for the devil's agents to shout it from the rooftops and be publicly humiliated? Most likely, any impurity in your life isn't so dramatic as the ones we read about in the newspapers. Most likely, it's merely character issues that God in His long-suffering is working out as you travel from glory to glory. But don't be deceived, God hates all sin, though He loves you with a passion. We must first separate the profane from the holy in our own lives, laying aside all self-righteousness, before we can humbly, yet boldly be used of the Holy Spirit as one who ushers in a spirit of conviction.

FUNCTIONING AS A PROPHET

Of course, there are many other aspects of prophetic ministry. Spiritual warfare, deliverance, understanding times and seasons, making decrees and announcements, encouraging the weak, being a watchman and issuing warnings, imparting spiritual gifts, confirming and activating, and foretelling and forthtelling. (If you are interested in solid prophetic training, pick up Jonas Clark's *Extreme Prophetic Studies*.[3])

Indeed, there are many aspects to prophetic ministry, and yet no two prophets are alike. God uses some prophets more in the area of foretelling and forthtelling. He uses others more in the area of warnings. He uses some more in the area of deliverance. Just like no two Christians are alike, no two prophets are alike. However, all prophets should have the same heartbeat. The foundation of prophetic ministry should be built on standing in the gap with intercessions, turning hearts to God, preparing a people to know and do His will, and separating the holy from the profane.

If our operations are in line with these fundamentals, then we will find safety. If our operations, rather, are based on a desire to gain recognition for foretelling and forthtelling, making decrees and announcements, and casting out demons, then we are missing the heart of the matter. Yes, we will do all those things and they are all valid operations of prophetic ministry. However, the operations of the prophetic ministry are not entirely the same in the Old and New Testaments. We must align ourselves with the heart of the prophetic under the order of Melchizedek so that all that flows from it is based on right motivations (Hebrews 5:10). New Testament prophets aren't functioning after the order of Aaron, the Levite. We are functioning under the same order as Jesus, the order of Melchizedek. It's misguided prophets who aren't flowing in that order who are hijacking prophetic ministry.

PROPHETIC KEYS

+ What you have to keep in mind when you look at the heart of the prophetic in New Testament times is the covenant. Jesus Christ is the Prophet and He is our prototype.

+ Old Testament or New, you can't separate the prophet from prayer. It is the lifeblood of the prophetic because it is our connection with God and His will.

+ Another function of the prophetic ministry shared by prophets operating under both the old and new covenants is turning the hearts of the fathers toward the sons and the hearts of the sons toward the fathers.

+ You can't divide a reformation mindset from the prophetic. Prophets have reformation in their DNA. Their goal is to see God's best for people and nations and they take action to bring change, whether that is in the heart of man, in spiritual warfare, or in building efforts of some sort.

♦ Teaching the saints what they must do to prepare to receive the promise in the prophetic word by tapping into the Scriptures is one way to help ensure the heart of the people are turned to the heart of the Father. Teaching them how to maintain or respond to what the Lord says He has given them in a prophetic word is another. Teaching them to pray the word through is yet another. And teaching them to wage a good warfare with the prophetic word is still another.

♦ Preparing a people for the Lord, then, is preparing their spirit and their souls, their spirits to receive wisdom and revelation in the knowledge of Him and their soul to align with the Spirit.

♦ The heart of the prophetic ministry includes separating the holy from the profane.

We must first separate the holy from the profane in our own lives, laying aside all self-righteousness, before we can humbly, yet boldly be used of the Holy Spirit as one who ushers in a spirit of conviction.

Chapter 3

HIJACKING
THE PROPHETIC

And many false prophets will rise up and deceive and lead many into error. And the love of the great body of people will grow cold because of the multiplied lawlessness and iniquity, But he who endures to the end will be saved (Matthew 24:11-13 AMP).

D o you remember where you were when Islamic extremists hijacked two airplanes and flew into the World Trade Center? September 11, 2001 was a tragic wake-up call for the United States of America. Terrorists infiltrated the land years earlier, but the government was not paying close enough attention to the manifest signs of the Islamic holy war. Lost lives prove that the nation could not thwart the attack.

At some level, the Church of Jesus Christ has made the same mistake. In some circles, spiritual terrorists have hijacked the prophetic for their own bizarre purposes. Prophetic pirates have indeed infiltrated the Church, but perhaps we didn't know enough about true prophets to recognize the false ones. It's interesting to note many sources that trace the root of the term "hijack." It was originally used to describe a criminal's way of approaching their victims. The hijacker would say to a driver transporting goods: "Stick 'em up high, Jack!" Today's prophetic hijackers may not say "stick 'em up" but they are nonetheless robbing believers blind, or perhaps it's better said that they are robbing blind believers. I'm here to issue a wake up call to the Church so we can stop these prophetic hijackers from hindering God's work.

Just as Elijah confronted the prophets of Baal and Jezebel, the time is coming when God's New Testament mouthpieces will confront modern-day prophetic cults that have risen to hijack this vital ministry. The true will defy the false. The holy will challenge the profane. Until that day, spirits of divination, with a little help from the lust of the eyes, the lust of the flesh and the pride of life are working overtime to woo God's true prophetic ambassadors to the side of the same err.

It grieves me that spirits of perversion have already made inroads into some segments of the prophetic ministry, deceiving supposed mature prophetic voices with prophecies that go beyond the realm of simple error. Of course, every prophet misses it from time to time – and remember the goal of this book is to equip you to flow more accurately so that we can glorify Christ with our utterances. God forbid we bring shame on His name on an international platform. God forbid our actions or our utterances cause those who have not yet received a revelation of the restoration of the prophetic ministry to throw the baby out with the defiled bathwater.

Am I being overzealous? I think not. I was recently listening to an evangelical radio broadcast on a South Florida radio station. This was just after a prominent Christian figure prophesied doom and gloom over the United States. The guest on the show was a doctor of theology that proceeded to nullify the existence of modern-day prophetic ministry because, he said, "I have never met someone who called himself a prophet who didn't either try to get money out of your pocket or who had anything good to say. It's all doom and gloom."

QUESTIONABLE PROPHECIES

I frequently hear questionable prophesies. In fact, as editor of *The Voice* magazine people send me prophetic words that are pages and pages long with little useful inspiration. They send them because they are hoping to have them published. They want a platform, but *The Voice* is reserved for God's voice and we will not compromise in exchange for promises of big advertising contracts. God has plenty to say and so does the devil. Still, questionable prophecies do find a home on the Internet for the world to read, a perversion of the medium that God is using in a mighty way.

Yes, questionable prophecies have floated around the Body of Christ over the years with plenty of agreeing head-nodders from allied prophetic camps. Remember the Y2K prophecy? Prophetic books filled bookstore shelves pronouncing doom and gloom at the arrival of the year 2000. Of course, after January 1, 2000 arrived without the dramatic events prophesied by some, the bookstores couldn't give those publications away. But alas, plenty of greenbacks were already in the pockets of their authors. Those who fell prey to the fear-laced prophecies spent years eating up the massive collection of canned goods stored in their basements. Others were deceived by prophecies warning the saints to double their giving in 1999. If they didn't, the false prophecy claimed, they would not survive 2000. Hooey!

What about the prophecy stating Bill Clinton would lead the United States of America into righteousness? What about the prophecy that Russian Jews would make a mass exodus to escape another holocaust in the fall of 2000? What about prophecies that claimed a world dictator would rise up by 2003? What about prophecies that said a nuclear war would start on September 12, 2006 around the great river Euphrates? Remember all the hype promoting 88 reasons why Jesus would return in 1988? Oh, I almost forgot. What about the prophecies that claim certain states have divine authority to tear down the spirit of Jezebel over the nation? That's one I'd love to see come to pass, but it's just not Scriptural. My desk is full of these authors' failed predictions. In fact, it's overflowing.

SHIFTING SPIRITUAL INSPIRATIONS

I believe in prophetic ministry with every fiber of my being, and it grieves me when Christians all out reject it. But I must admit I can see why some are scared away. We've all received questionable personable prophecies, and they can admittedly be troubling if they tap into some insecurity in our souls. But I'm not talking about Jezebel in your local church who uses prophecy to control. I'm talking about questionable prophecies delivered to the Church at large. I am talking about prophetic utterances that seem ridiculous from the get-go but find broad acceptance in some prophetic camps. I am talking about the inability to separate the holy from the profane.

I don't have all the answers as to why this happens, but I can only come to one conclusion: The prophet is not in full alignment with the Chief Cornerstone. Jesus was never deceived and the more closely we align ourselves with Him the less chance there is we will be deceived. We'll never be perfect so long as we are clothed in this flesh, but I believe if we don't continually work out our salvation with fear and trembling, if we don't walk in a fear of the Lord, if we don't maintain a humility before God and man, then we are open targets for deception. The Apostle James warned that if we are hearers of the Word but not doers, we are self-deceived.

Like you, I don't want to be deceived. I don't want to fall into the trap Peter fell into where one moment He was speaking under divine revelation and the next moment he was speaking under the inspiration of the devil. I know you don't, either. I don't believe anyone does, but there comes a temptation so great that only those who are completely submitted to the will of God and willing to sacrifice all at His command can avoid it. The danger is great. There are even a few who were so overcome by deception they thought they were the resurrected Old Testament Prophet Elijah. If it can happen to others, it can happen to you.

THREE TYPES OF PROPHETS

A more common issue in some prophetic circles falls short of questionable prophecies and goes beyond the pale of the prophetic to reach occult status. There are prophetic cults rising in the Body of Christ who are deceiving and being deceived (2 Timothy 3:13). And should we be surprised? The Bible warns of false prophets over and again. Just as true prophets travel and minister in companies, wouldn't it stand to reason that false prophets would, too? If you need further evidence, just read I Kings. There you will find two companies of false prophets: the Baal prophets and the Jezebel prophets. In fact, you'll only find three

types of prophets mentioned in the Old Testament
– the prophets of Baal, the prophets of Jezebel and the
prophets of Jehovah.

1. PROPHETS OF BAAL

Let me take you on a little bunny trail so you can see
the differences. Baal is a god of prophetic divination.
This spirit leads people into idolatry just like it led
the Israelites into idolatry when Moses was on the
mountain talking with God. Remember when the
children of Israel made a molten calf as an idol to
worship? That was the spirit of Baal (Exodus 32:8).
Prophets of Baal, then, offer prophetic utterances that
lead you into idolatry. In other words, they lead you
away from God to some selfish motive in your own heart.

What is idolatry? It's when you put something
above God in your life. It's when you are more
devoted to something than God. That could be a job,
a relationship, money, etc. So prophets of Baal use
divination to tap into the idolatry in your own heart
and prophesy what they find there through familiar
spirits. Listen now, if you go to a meeting and a prophet
announces a special prayer line for all those who sow

$1,000 in exchange for a financial breakthrough, a powerful prayer life, a restored relationship, or anything of the like, then you are in the midst of Baal's camp. The Baal prophets network together and invite each other to their churches to merchandise their own sheep. They join together for mega fundraisers that leave the sowers with empty pockets that won't be filled with anything other than the wrong motives they came to the altar with.

2. PROPHETS OF JEZEBEL

The spirit of Ashtoreth influences the prophets of Jezebel. Ashtoreth was the pagan god Queen Jezebel served. Ashtoreth was known as a seducing goddess of war. This is a different camp than the Baal prophets – and with a different motive. The prophets of Jezebel prophesy smooth flattering words to manipulate and control. If that doesn't work, they transition into warfare mode and prophesy fearful sayings to control you. When you hear prophetic judgments and curses that are clearly not coming from the heart of God, you are dealing with one of Jezebel's modern-day prophets. Just like Queen Jezebel released fearful death threats in the Old Testament, New Testament prophets consumed with the spirit of Jezebel continue to release fearful death threats in the form of judgments and curses. Ashtoreth and Baal were married. So these spirits often share one another's characteristics. We must discern what we are dealing with.

3. PROPHETS OF JEHOVAH

The third type of prophet, of course, is Jehovah's prophets. In the New Testament, these are the Melchizedek prophets. New Testament prophets are not serving under the order of Aaron. They are serving under the order of Melchizedek just as Jesus did (Hebrews 5). Jesus, our prototype Prophet, will not tolerate the spirit of Jezebel (control and manipulation through flattery and fear) nor will He condone Baal worship (idolatry). If Jesus doesn't tolerate these spirits, we should not tolerate them either. We must first look to our own hearts to purge ourselves of any common ground we may have with these wicked spirits. Then we can begin to confront these dark powers and set captives free from the grip of deception.

THE RISE OF PROPHETIC CULTS

Some have said that God is releasing an army of prophets in these last days. I agree. I'd add this: He is raising strong prophetic churches full of the Spirit of God and equipped believers who are wise and understand the will of the Lord (Ephesians 5). That's what it's going to take to combat the rise of prophetic cults who consort with Baal and Jezebel to push their agenda under the guise of prophetic intercession. Let me just repeat that in a different way. We need to hit that devil again. We need strong believers to stand up and speak out against false prophetic cults who portend to be calling the nation to intercession but are actually leading people down a path that leads to destruction. We need not call these false prophetic cults out by name. Instead, we can call out the practice so Christians who have not been trained in prophetic ministry won't be deceived and miss out on God's best for their lives by getting caught up in this flow.

The Body of Christ will always need prophets, not to do the hearing from God for believers, rather to equip believers to hear and understand the will of the Lord for themselves so they are not tossed to and fro by every wind of doctrine (Ephesians 4). Controlling prophets don't want believers to hear from God for themselves because they would lose control. So they band together, nodding in agreement with one another's bitterness-backed prophecies and make a name for themselves with some help from the prince of the power of the air. Simply put, they form prophetic cults. I'm not talking about folks like David Koresh or Jim Jones that lead their followers into suicide. I'm talking about those who are tapping into Kabbalah (sometimes also called Qabalah, Kabbala or Cabala). The word literally means "receiving" and it is deceiving because its practitioners are not hearing from the Spirit of God. In essence, the way some prophets are exploiting Kabbalah amounts to demonic mysticism.

Those who prophesy with the guide of Kabbalah believe mastering this "receiving" will bring them spiritually closer to God. They use Kabbalah to prophesy and even control nature. (That would explain all the prophetic judgments about natural disasters, like hurricanes, tsunamis, fires and earthquakes, wouldn't it? Consider that Baal is the god of rain, thunder, fertility and agriculture, the picture becomes even clearer.) I don't have time in this book to outline all the beliefs of Kabbalah, but here are a couple of quick tenets that will clue you in to its goings on in the Body of Christ when you see it.

First, Kabbalah teaches Hebrew symbols, numbers, letters and words – even the accents on the words – offer a hidden meaning. It also teaches its practitioners dozens of ways to interpret these meanings, but it's easiest explained by the way it takes numerical values of words and adds them up, then offers a key to reveal supposed hidden meanings in Scripture. Let me just say this: Jesus didn't say Kabbalah would lead and guide us into all truth. He promised the Holy Spirit would fill that role in His absence (John 16:13). Any other guide is strictly forbidden.

SELL ME YOUR SECRET

Baal prophets are infused with the spirit of idolatry. That's the "self" spirit we'll discuss in more detail later. We also know people who are in bondage to the spirit of Jezebel often resort to control and manipulation to protect themselves from fresh hurts and wounds. I believe the root of prophetic cults – and any other type of cult – is bitterness. And it seems the only thing that soothes their pain is power, money, fame and celebrity. What makes me think that, you ask? Scripture's chronicle of Simon the sorcerer.

"Simon had practiced magic in the city, posing as a famous man and dazzling all the Samaritans with his wizardry. He had them all, from little children to old men, eating out of his hand. They all thought he had supernatural powers, and called him 'the Great Wizard.' He had been around a long time and everyone was more or less in awe of him" (Acts 8:9-11 MSG).

Here we learn old Simon the sorcerer was an imposter. He reveled in the attention the townspeople showered upon him. The King James translation of Verse 10 reveals how the people respected him: "This man has the great power of God." So we see that Simon was a false prophet who had gained the trust of the people and probably called in financial favors in exchange for his mystical powers. The fact that Simon had money in his pocket and thought it was convenient to buy and sell "power" is evidenced by a visit from the apostles Peter and John.

Philip's preaching apparently got Simon born again because the Bible says, "Simon himself believed also and was baptized (Acts 8:13.) After his conversion, he continued following Philip and observing the miracles and signs that were wrought at his hand. Then the apostles Peter and John showed up and brought the baptism of the Holy Ghost with them. They laid their hands on the people and these newly minted disciples freely received the Holy Spirit and the power that comes along with Him. Simon was awestruck by the demonstration of power at the hands of the apostles. He was amazed that the believers were speaking in other tongues and prophesying. That's about the time Simon made his dreadful mistake. He offered the apostles money in exchange for Holy Ghost power (Acts 8:18-19). He was met with a sharp rebuke from Peter.

> "When Simon saw that the apostles by merely laying on hands conferred the Spirit, he pulled out his money, excited, and said, 'Sell me your secret! Show me how you did that! How much do you want? Name your price!' Peter said, 'To hell with your money! And you along with it. Why, that's unthinkable—trying to buy God's gift! You'll never be part of what God is doing by striking bargains and offering bribes. Change your ways—and now! Ask the Master to forgive you for trying to use God to make money. I can see this is an old habit with you; you reek with money-lust'" (Acts 8:18-23 MSG).

Ouch! The King James translation gets to the root of the matter. Peter says, "I perceive that thou art in the gall of bitterness, and in the bond of iniquity" (Acts 8:23). Gall is bile, that yellow-green viscid alkaline fluid the liver secrets and passes to the intestines. In other words, it goes to the gut. You could say Simon had a root of bitterness in his life. Bitterness is associated with unforgiveness after a severe hurt or wound that hasn't healed. Who knows what happened to Simon, who rejected him or hurt him? But being an occultist power-wielding big shot made him feel better about himself. When he got born again, he knew he had to put away his occultist powers but his ego still needed a lift, so he sought to buy the power of God and keep the people eating out of the palms of his hands.

The Apostle James made it clear: a fountain can't put forth sweet and bitter water (James 3:11). Rejection, hurts and wounds – and the bitterness that may result in the wake of unforgiveness of the ones who caused them – can lead someone into prophetic divination. If misery loves company, then it's easy to see how companies of false prophets, A.K.A. prophetic cults, would wind up mingling together. I've talked to members in some prophetic cults. They pump each other's egos in every conversation. They spew forth prophecies that tap into the idolatry of people's hearts in prayer lines and prophesy judgments and curses out of the bitterness of their own – and they make money in the process. God loves these people yet their self-deception surely grieves Him. What's important to remember is something in the heart of these false prophetic ministers opened the door to the devil's seeds. That's why we must continually ask God to create in us a clean heart and be sensitive to His prompting to repent and renew our minds.

Unfortunately, there is no denying that the spirit of Jezebel has already hijacked some segments of the prophetic ministry. Like a terrorist who extorts, swindles or coerces a pilot at gunpoint, the Jezebel spirit is kidnapping prophets who have unresolved character issues, bitterness, hurts and wounds and using them for sinister purposes. I've said it before and I'll keep saying it. I don't believe false prophets start out as false prophets. I believe they go astray somewhere on the road to Christ-likeness. We need prophets and intercessors that hear the Spirit accurately and can stand in the ministries they've been called to with integrity. The good news is there are more who are than who aren't, and even if you have fallen into this ditch you can repent and get back on track. In the next chapter we'll begin looking at some of the potholes that derail this vital ministry.

PROPHETIC KEYS

+ Jesus was never deceived and the more closely we align ourselves with Him the less chance that we will be deceived. We'll never be perfect, but I believe if we don't continually work out our salvation with fear and trembling, if we don't walk in a fear of the Lord, if we don't maintain humility before God and man, then we are open targets for deception.

+ If you go to a meeting where a prophet announces a special prayer line for all those who sow $1,000 in exchange for a financial breakthrough, a powerful prayer life, a restored relationship, or anything of the like, then you are in the midst of Baal's camp.

+ The prophets of Jezebel prophesy smooth flattering words to manipulate and control. If that doesn't work, they transition into warfare mode and prophesy fearful sayings to control you.

♦ Jesus didn't say Kabbalah would lead and guide us into all truth. He promised the Holy Spirit would fill that role in His absence (John 16:13). Any other guide is strictly forbidden.

♦ What's important to remember is something in the heart of these false prophetic ministers opened the door to the devil's seeds. That's why we must continually ask God to create in us a clean heart and be sensitive to His prompting to repent and renew our minds.

Chapter 4

THE POLITICALLY CORRECT PROPHET

Elijah challenged the people: 'How long are you going to sit on the fence? If God is the real God, follow him; if it's Baal, follow him. Make up your minds!' Nobody said a word; nobody made a move. (1 Kings 18:21 MSG)

There's a highly contagious and lethal virus running rampant in the world. Sadly, it's even made its way into some circles of the prophetic ministry. That virus is called "political correctness" and it threatens to pervert the voice of God.

The origins of this phrase are argued, but many believe "politically correct" has its roots in Marxist-Leninist vocabulary as a term used to describe the party line. (The party line includes the principles or policies of an individual or organization.) Whether it's a Marxist term or not, you know a mindset has gone mainstream when it makes its way into the dictionary. The very definition of politically correct defies prophets. This adjective describes the act of conforming to a belief that languages and practices which could offend political sensibilities (as in matters of sex or race) should be eliminated.[4]

My God…That would mean no more John the Baptist, who called a sin a sin. It would mean no more Jeremiah, who spoke the word of the Lord despite persecution. It would mean no more Jesus, too, because tolerance has in many places taken the place of righteousness. Jesus loves and died for all, but the religious spirit behind many "politically correct" motives is troublesome and prophets and intercessors must not bow to it. The only party line the Christian prophet should be toeing is the Kingdom party, which is neither a democratic government nor a humanistic venture.

In the world, political correctness is behind such popular new words as "herstory" which attempts to take the male element out of "his-story." Or what about

THE POLITICALLY CORRECT PROPHET

the man in the Glasgow coffee shop who couldn't get his morning 'black coffee' until he changed the verbiage in his request to 'coffee without milk'? And what about the BBC's attempt to strip away the truth from the London Tube bombings by calling terrorists "misguided criminals"?

In the Church, political correctness publishes an 'inclusive' Bible to replace what it deems as divisive teachings of Christianity with oft-heretical terms. Case in point, the Lord's prayer was changed to "Our Mother and Father Who are in Heaven." The Anglican Church at Cardiff Cathedral in Wales changed the 500-year-old song "God Rest Ye Merry Gentlemen" to "God Rest Ye Merry Persons." (See the Global Language Monitor[5] for additional examples.) Political correctness also offers people titles and front row seats based on tenure rather than God-ordained roles and ministries.

Call me 'politically incorrect' and I'll thank you for the compliment. My aim is not to offend anyone, but c'mon prophets. If the choice is between offending God and offending man, who would you choose to offend? (Hint: the 'godly correct' answer would be to offend man.) If we are doing the work of the ministry, we are bound to offend someone. Nevertheless, we have to commit our mouths to God like Isaiah did (Isaiah

6:5-8). We may please some of the people some of the time, but we have to please God all of the time.

Elijah threw down the gauntlet in the face of an Israeli generation that was sitting on the fence of non-committal. The prophet told the people to make up their minds who they would serve: Jehovah or Baal. Since a double-minded man is unstable in all his ways (James 1:8), fence-sitting Christians face the danger of crossing the boundary marker that separates loyalty to God from befriending the world. The latter is adulterous. Do you not know that being the world's friend equates to being God's enemy? Whoever chooses to be a friend of the world takes his stand as an enemy of God (James 4:4).

Consider the gauntlet thrown down. I am throwing it down with righteous fervor in hopes of helping others see this virus that's infecting prophetic ministry with spiritual death. Indeed, if there is political correctness in our characters, we may succumb to the fear of man – and we all know that we can't flow in the fear of man and the fear of God at the same time. Political correctness opens the door for the religious spirit to flow in our lives and that adulterates the pure flow that God needs in order to get His message out to a dying world. It's one thing to be polite and tell someone their bad hair cut isn't all that bad. (The truth is the hair will grow back, so it's not all that bad.) It's another thing to be politically correct about issues that touch God's heart, like sin of any and every kind. We can't water down God's word – logos or rhema – and call ourselves prophets.

PICTURE OF THE P.C. PROPHET

What does a P.C. prophet look like? The P.C. prophet is one who will not cross the party line. If God says something that may stir controversy in the P.C. prophet's circle of friends, the mouthpiece won't pipe up. If the prophetic utterance could negatively impact the P.C. prophet's pocketbook, the prophecy will remain hidden in a drawer. Political correctness is a bacteria that breeds perversion in the prophetic. It causes a disease that can be fatal to prophetic ministry if left unchecked. Like David, we must hate what God hates (Psalm 139:21-22). True prophets have mercy gifts, yes, but mercy and political correctness are drawn from different wells. We are not to bring judgment upon sinners, but we are not to condone sin, either. We must reverence God, love the sinner, and despise the sin.

T. Austin Sparks (1888-1971), a native Londoner and author of "Prophetic Ministry: A Classic Study on the Nature of a Prophet"[6] painted this picture of a prophet: "A true prophet, like Samuel, will be charitable as long as possible, until that wrong thing takes the pronounced and positive form of disobedience to light given…Samuel showed a great deal of forbearance with things that were wrong, even while in his heart he could not accept them. He hoped light would break and obedience follow and the situation be saved."

God's prophets must not compromise. Whatever the Spirit of God is saying to the Church, that is what we must say to the Church. We must not change a jot or tittle (Matthew 5:18). We must not dilute the message to suit the hearers. We must not hold back for fear of what man will do to us. You might think, "I would never do that." Maybe you wouldn't. Or maybe you would and you just don't know it. Sometimes we don't know what we'd do until the test comes. Ultimately, it's between you and the Holy Ghost. I encourage you to ask Him and He will show you if you have a bent toward political correctness.

The bottom line is political correctness that compromises the Word of truth is a prophetic pothole we need to avoid. Again, if you see these tendencies in your soul, it probably stems from one of two sources: fear of man or a religious spirit with undue influence in your life. Let's take a look at each of these ungodly influencers that tries to get us to compromise what says the Spirit of God.

OF WHOM SHALL
YOU BE AFRAID?

Fear of man is one of the culprits behind the political correctness that has seeped into the Church of Jesus Christ. Jesus, the Prophet, wasn't politically correct. He called a Pharisee a Pharisee and pronounced woe on the religious spirit-motivated hypocrites of His day. Jesus had no fear of man, nor was He a respecter of persons. I dare say if Jesus was politically correct we'd all be in trouble. I can't imagine a politically correct Savior making it all the way to the cross with so many opportunities to compromise with Pharisees, Sadducees, Herodians, and even the masses who wanted to crown Him King in a natural revolution.

Fear of man can cause us to fall into a politically correct trap, if there is such a thing. The P.C. camp probably wouldn't call it a trap. They'd call it a "temporary fence of protection" or some other thinned term. Listen, fear of man will prevent us from prophesying the will of the Lord. If we are concerned about what people will think of us, then how can we deliver a word boldly? Let me field that question on your behalf: We can't. If we aren't willing to deliver the unadulterated word of the Lord in spite of the persecution it will bring us, then we will never get to the level of prophesying over governments and nations. And even if we did we wouldn't stay there. The devil would take us out when we'd served his purpose. Let's look at another path. Just as fear of man causes politically correct prophets to shrink back from the disapproval of one's colleagues, an absence of a fear of the Lord causes "judgment prophets" to boldly declare curses over them. Interesting contrast, isn't it? We'll take a closer look at the judgment-and-curse pitfall later in the book. For now, remember the wisdom of the preacher, who offered a contrast we should all take to heart when tempted with the fear of man and people-pleasing: "The fear of man brings a snare: but whoever leans on, trusts in, and puts his confidence in the Lord is safe and set on high" (Proverbs 29:25 AMP). Solomon sounds just like his dad, David, who declared, "The Lord is on my side; I will not fear. What can man do to me?" (Psalm 118:6)

SAMUEL'S INTRODUCTION
TO THE PROPHETIC

Again, Jesus, the Prophet, wasn't politically correct. Although he was not disrespectful to the Law of Moses or the law of the land, he did not allow these edicts to override God's perfect will. He called a Pharisee a Pharisee and He put them in their place over and over with the wisdom of God in boldness. Jesus didn't fear the Pharisees. He didn't fear the multitudes. He didn't fear the false prophets. He didn't fear the devil himself. Jesus was fully dependent on His Father and He demonstrated faith in the face of every obstacle. The Bible says we prophesy according to our faith (Romans 12:6). Faith and love overcome fear. If we believe the Lord truly spoke to us, then we will be less likely to fall into the snare of the fear of man. Fear of man leaves us susceptible to being controlled and manipulated by political correctness at the sake of God's will.

Let's compare the responses of two Biblical characters in the light of the fear of man and the political correctness that often results. Comparing and contrasting the Prophet Samuel with King Saul offers a clear view of where the path of boldness and the path of compromise can take us.

We know the boy Samuel ministered before the Lord under the authority of Eli. In those days the prophetic word of the Lord was rare. There were not many visions. One night, young Samuel was lying in the temple, minding his own business, and the Lord called him. You know the story. Samuel didn't immediately recognize the call. The Bible says he did not yet know the Lord (1 Samuel 3:4-8). How many of us are like that? God is calling us to do something and we respond inappropriately because we just aren't sure it was really God. Our hearts are right, but it takes us longer to get in line with God's will because we are unfamiliar with the way the Lord is moving. We do not yet know the Lord in that way.

Eli did know the ways of the Lord. So the third time Samuel came running in obedience to what he thought was Eli's beckoning, the old dim-eyed priest caught on to what was happening and told the boy what to do. Thank God that in our obedient ignorance His mercy continues to reach out to us. When God called Samuel a fourth time he responded, "Speak, Lord, for your servant is listening." Then the Lord told young Samuel some disturbing news that may have made him wish he had rolled over and plugged his ears. The Lord told Samuel,

"I will carry out against Eli everything I spoke against his family – from beginning to end. For I told him that I would judge his family forever because of the sin he knew about; his sons made themselves contemptible, and he failed to restrain them. Therefore, I swore to the house of Eli, 'The guilt of Eli's house will never be atoned for by sacrifice or offering'" (1 Samuel 3:11-14 NIV).

SAMUEL'S SERIOUS STRUGGLE

That was Samuel's introduction to the prophetic. His first prophetic insight came with a major test because the Lord had no time to waste. He needed to raise a prophet in the land and He had chosen Samuel. I can just imagine how Samuel spent the rest of the night, pondering over the word of the Lord with sorrow. Eli was his spiritual father, the only consistent authority figure in his life. I'm sure Samuel loved Eli as such. The Bible says Samuel lay down until morning and then opened the doors of the house of the Lord. I bet he didn't sleep a wink. I bet he hoped Eli wouldn't ask him if the Lord came calling again. I bet he wished he could pull the covers over his head and just stay in bed. But he performed his regular service, with great fear.

The Bible says Samuel was afraid to tell Eli the vision, but Eli called him and said, "Samuel, my son." Of course, Samuel answered, "Here I am." Then Eli asked the youth what the Lord had said. He was scared to tell Eli what the Lord showed him, but the man of God issued an edict: "Don't hide it from me. May God deal with you, be it ever so severely, if you hide from me anything He told you" (1 Samuel 3:17). Here is the valley of quick decision. The Bible doesn't offer up how long it took Samuel to respond. Maybe he just blurted out what the Lord said and got it over with. Maybe he stammered and hem hawed in fear. But his ultimate choice was clear: He could respond in the fear of man or the fear of the Lord.

Ultimately, Samuel was more fearful of the Lord's wrath than Eli's potentially angry response. He knew that Eli could make his life miserable if he chose to, but Eli's edict inviting the Lord's hand into the matter opened Samuel's eyes to a greater consequence: God's discipline for keeping silent. That needs to be our position. Samuel passed the test. And we know that God trusted Samuel. He never succumbed to that politically correct spirit, although he had opportunities through the course of his ministry. Samuel was a

God-pleaser, not a man-pleaser, and God continued to promote him.

OBEDIENCE IS BETTER THAN SACRIFICE

King Saul had a true ministry and anointing from God, but the fear of man and a people-pleasing spirit that influenced his life led him to a counterfeit spiritual authority. Saul had a promising start. He was 30 years old when he became king. He was a mighty warrior, but he found himself in a compromising position that led him to compromise the will of the Lord in due course. Just like lying, one compromise often seems to lead to another, then another, then another. For Saul that compromise led him to the witch's house.

Let's pick up Saul's story at the scene of battle. The Philistines assembled to fight Israel with 3,000 chariots, 6,000 charioteers, and soldiers as numerous as the sand on the seashore. They went up and camped at Michmash, east of Beth Aven. When the men of Israel saw their situation was critical and their army was hard pressed, they hid in caves and thickets, among the rocks, and in pits and cisterns. Some Hebrews even crossed the Jordan to the land of Gad and Gilead. Saul showed a little more courage, though he was clearly in a compromising position. He remained at Gilgal, and all the troops with him were quaking with fear.

Saul waited seven days, the time set by Samuel; but Samuel did not come to Gilgal, and Saul's men began to scatter. This is the event that marked the beginning of the end for Saul. It was Saul's test and, unlike Samuel, he failed it miserably. Instead of continuing to wait for Samuel, Saul told his men to bring him the burnt offering and the fellowship offerings. Of course, Saul was not a priest and it was not his duty to perform this ceremony. He was disobedient to the Lord in more ways than one. Wouldn't you know it, just as soon as Saul had fallen into snare of the fear of man Samuel finally showed up.

When Samuel asked Saul what in the world he had done, Saul said, "Because I saw that the people were scattered from me, and that thou camest not within the days appointed, and that the Philistines gathered themselves together at Michmash; Therefore said I, The Philistines will come down now upon me to Gilgal, and I have not made supplication unto the Lord: I forced myself therefore, and offered a burnt offering" (I Samuel 13:11-12). Saul said he forced himself. But what he really did was give in to the pressure of the fear of man. He made the offering prematurely because he feared the people would leave him. It was the fear of man, not the fear of the Lord that caused him to disobey. Obedience is the best way to maintain the favor of the Lord. The Bible says obedience is better than sacrifice (I Samuel 15:22).

THE DOOR TO DIVINATION

Saul could have seen a mighty breakthrough in his life, but he let man-pleasing get the best of him. Samuel called his actions foolish and told him as much. Samuel explained to Saul that his kingdom could have been established upon Israel forever. Now it would not endure (1 Samuel 13:13-14). The hunt was on for Saul's replacement. Yet Israel's first king would go on to win battles in the name of the Lord for a time – a short time. Just two chapters later, Saul's first compromise led to a second, more fateful one. The Lord spoke through Samuel with a battle command for Saul to utterly destroy the Amalekites. Saul went up to battle, but spared the king and kept the best of the sheep, cattle, calves and lambs. He was unwilling to destroy the goods of the land. This grieved the Lord and sent Samuel into deep intercession for the king (1 Samuel 15:7-10).

Saul fell into the same compromise because of what was in him. That politically correct, man-fearing, people-pleasing spirit got the best of him and he disobeyed God. Samuel rebuked Saul for his partial obedience. Partial obedience, my friends, is rebellion and that's exactly what Samuel called it:

> "For rebellion is as the sin of witchcraft, and stubbornness is as iniquity and idolatry. Because thou hast rejected the word of the Lord, he hath also rejected thee from being king" (1 Samuel 15:23).

Saul was stripped of his kingship. Of course, he still had the position of king. But the anointing on his life was gone. Listen up, prophets. The gifts and callings of God are indeed without repentance (Romans 11:29). You may very well keep your title of Prophet So-and-So and continue to bask in the praise of men for a season. But I submit to you that the anointing on your life will wane. You can't carry a strong anointing in sheer disobedience to the Lord. I once heard a man of God say, "The Lord anoints purpose." That means it's not about you. It's about God's purpose in you. If you aren't fulfilling your purpose, why would God anoint you? Why would He anoint a politically correct prophet who flows in the fear of man and refuses to speak His word without compromise? That's a rhetorical question, of course. He doesn't and He won't.

Now, before we move on, consider Samuel's admonishment to Saul. He said rebellion is as the sin of witchcraft. Fast-forward to Chapter 28, which in real time was many years later. Samuel has gone on to be with the Lord. Saul is still fighting the Philistines, and he was still afraid when he saw their number. Saul was desperate and, despite his oft disobedience to the Lord, wanted His help. So Saul inquired of the Lord. The Lord did not answer him, neither by dreams, nor by Urim, nor by the prophets.

Instead of pressing in to God, Saul made yet another compromise as he headed to a woman with a familiar spirit in Endor to get some spiritual guidance. Unfortunately for Saul, he didn't like what he heard: He would die in battle the next day, his last act of compromise having led him to the witch's house (1 Samuel 28). Here's the moral of the story: If we receive our authority, recognition or security from men we could end up like Saul – in the the den of divination. Don't fall into the trap of political correctness. Politics is risky business. God's way is secure.

REVEALING
RELIGIOUS MANIFESTOS

So how do you tell if you are flowing in religion or political correctness? Ask yourself if you are building walls of religion or towers of prayer? Your answer could denote the difference between a woe-filled fate and a fulfilled destiny. If you are seeking titles and positions for the admiration of men, then you are at risk of falling prey to the religious spirit. The spirit of religion attempts to block the Holy Spirit's work, conform people into compromising believers, and put on a show, among other ungodly maneuvers, according to Apostle Jonas Clark, my spiritual father and mentor. In his book, "30 Pieces of Silver" he describes many of the operations of a religious spirit. Let's take a quick look at his description of religious politics [7]:

> "Religious spirits are the best players of religious politics, which is the quiet killer of both ministries and churches today. To advance their political agenda, religious spirits will join whatever opinion is religiously correct at the time... Through the eyes of a religious spirit, everything is seen as a political ladder...

They spend a lot of time thinking thoughts like, 'What do I have to say, do or act like in order to advance me, my, and mine to the top of the ladder of this church or ministry?' Unfortunately for them, they will find out that their ladder is leaning against the wrong wall."

With these words of experiential wisdom in mind, can you see the affect the religious spirit might have on a prophet? Prophets are called alongside apostles to build the local church. But the religious spirit is the silent killer of ministries. Prophets are called to advance God's agenda, but the religious spirit has its own agenda. Prophets are called to walk in humility, but the religious spirit walks in pride (or false humility which has the same root). Prophets are called to speak forth the mind and will of God, but the religious spirit seeks to manipulate in order to gain the admiration of men through position seeking. Our position is in Christ. Yes, titles are necessary to describe functions in the Body of Christ, but if we are letting the quest for a title or position influence our prophetic utterances then we have sorely missed the mark.

NO WHITEWASH, PLEASE!

True prophets are not always the most popular five-fold ministry gift on the block because they are bold enough to release a word of the Lord that deals with sin or warns of potentially unpleasant circumstances coming down the proverbial pike. Prophets obsessed by the fear of man or unholy desires will not fulfill God's ultimate plan. We must be careful, then, not to prophesy according to the party line in order to establish and preserve popularity in ministry circuits. If we fall into this trap we find ourselves in danger of perverting the gift of God by building walls of religion.

Politically correct prophets build walls of religion that lead people astray with fabricated edification, misleading exhortation and counterfeit comfort.

"These evil prophets deceive my people saying, 'All is peaceful!' when there is no peace at all! It's as if the people have built a flimsy wall, and these prophets are trying to hold it together by covering it with whitewash! Tell these whitewashers that their wall will soon fall down" (Ezekiel 13:10 NLT).

You can't whitewash sin. You can't whitewash religion. And you can't whitewash political correctness. We must guard our hearts in order to maintain a pure prophetic flow and a life of prayer that will wash away the plans of the enemy instead of fortifying his deception by watering down the truth for the sake of acceptance.

IT'S NOT A POPULARITY CONTEST

True prophets may not always have the flare, charisma or appeal of their politically correct counterparts, but who said they are supposed to? Jeremiah wasn't the most popular prophet in his time, nor was Ezekiel in his day. John the Baptist had his head served up on a silver platter for warning the people of the looming decision between everlasting life and eternal hellfire. But they were the unadulterated mouthpieces of God. And so it should be.

Anyone carrying a prophetic mantle needs to closely examine the fruit of his or her ministry. If we have prophesied peace unto popularity, then we need to repent. We need to trade in our whitewash for some spiritual mortar and start building towers of prayer that will bring genuine edification, authentic exhortation and legitimate comfort to God's people.

Let us not be foolish prophets who build our ministries on the sands of seduction for the sake of acceptance. Jehovah promises rain will pour from the heavens, hailstones will come hurtling down and violent winds will burst forth against those whitewashed walls and you will be exposed (Ezekiel 13:11-12). Instead, let us build our ministries on the Rock and prophesy the mind of Christ so when the hurricanes of religion come against the local church and when Jezebel hurls her spiritual sleet at the sanctuary, and when winds of witchcraft blow against the walls, the foundation of our ministries and our local churches will be fortified to stand and withstand in the day of battle.

AVOIDING P.C. STATUS

Prophets and intercessors need to avoid P.C. status like the plague. If you've fallen into the snare of political correctness, be it by way of the fear of man, a religious spirit, or some other factor, then you need to get a new perspective. Listen, fear of man is a major temptation. That's why God called prophets into ministry with a quick warning not to fear. God told Jeremiah not to be afraid of their faces (Jeremiah 1:4-9). He told Ezekiel not to be afraid of them or their words (Ezekiel 2:6). In other words, ignore the persecution in whatever form it comes.

The only way to avoid P.C. status is by trusting completely in God. Read Psalm 37. It always encourages me not to fret over evildoers, both in the Church and in the world, and to continue to do good. At the same time, I take seriously Jesus' command to pray for my enemies, to love them, to bless those who curse me, to do good to those who hate me, to pray for those who mistreat me and persecute me (Matthew 5:44). Being a doer of the Word guards your heart from anger, rejection, bitterness and the malice that ride on the back of persecution.

God called Abram, the first prophet mentioned in the Bible, "friend." I beseech you by the mercies of God to be a friend to God and choose to serve Him fully instead of tapping into the ways of the world. Be like the Prophet Abram, who refused to compromise with the wicked king of Sodom. The riches of compromise are deceitful riches that will lead you out of God's will. Repeat the words of Abram in the face of those who offer rewards in exchange for compromise:

"I have raised my hand to the Lord, God Most High, Creator of heaven and earth, and have taken an oath that I will accept nothing belonging to you, not even a thread or the thong of a sandal, so that you will never be able to say, 'I made Abram rich'" (Genesis 14:22-23).

PROPHETIC KEYS

+ The very definition of politically correct defies prophets. This adjective describes the act of conforming to a belief that languages and practices which could offend political sensibilities (as in matters of sex or race) should be eliminated.

+ The only way to avoid P.C. status is to trust completely in God. Being a doer of the Word guards your heart from anger, rejection, bitterness and the malice that ride on the back of persecution.

+ Political correctness opens the door for the religious spirit to flow in our lives and that adulterates the pure flow that God needs to get His message out to a dying world.

+ Listen, fear of man will prevent us from prophesying the will of the Lord. If we are concerned about what people will think of us, then how can we deliver a word boldly?

+ Prophets are called alongside apostles to build the local church. But the religious spirit is the silent killer of ministries. Prophets are called to advance God's agenda, but the religious spirit has its own agenda. Prophets are called to walk in humility, but the religious spirit walks in pride.

+ If you've fallen into the snare of political correctness, be it by way of fear of man, a religious spirit, or some other factor, then you just need to get a new perspective.

+ The riches of compromise are deceitful riches that will lead you out of God's will.

Chapter 5

THE PRESUMPTUOUS PROPHET

When a prophet speaketh in the name of the Lord, if the thing follow not, nor come to pass, that is the thing which the Lord hath not spoken, but the prophet hath spoken it presumptuously: thou shalt not be afraid of him (Deuteronomy 18:22).

As we continue to pursue the heart of the prophetic, let's be cautious about flowing in presumption. Remember the famous greeting, "Dr. Livingstone, I presume?"

Many of you have heard the story of Henry Stanley, the ambitious American reporter who went to the Dark

Continent in search of Dr. David Livingstone, a 19th century missionary who explored sub-Saharan Africa.

Stanley finally tracked down the famed evangelist. His first words when approaching the only other white man in Ujiji, Africa were, as the story goes, "Dr. Livingstone, I presume?" The white man's identity may have seemed like a no-brainer to the young journalist, but if he had been a prophet Stanley's presumption would have landed him in a heap of trouble. That's because presumption is on God's blacklist.

What does it literally mean to presume? And what exactly is presumption? When you presume you form an opinion from little or no evidence. Presumption also means to take as true or as fact without actual proof. Presumptuous could also mean "to overstep due bounds" and "to take liberties." Those definitions[8] outline some critical prophetic dos and don'ts that we'll discuss in this chapter so we can steer clear of this poisonous pitfall. We'll get back to Stanley later.

PROPHETIC PREJUDICE?

I noticed something interesting while studying about presumption. The definition of "presume" and the definition of "prejudice" are extremely similar and closer reflection offers up some important insights into the poison of presumption. Remember, presume means to form an opinion from little or no evidence and to take something as true or as fact without actual proof. Well, wait until you hear this. Some definitions of the word "prejudice"[9] include a "preconceived judgment or opinion or an adverse opinion or leaning formed without just grounds or before sufficient knowledge."

Hmm. Sounds at least a little bit like a religious spirit to me. Wasn't it those Pharisees that judged Jesus for healing on the Sabbath day and doing all other sorts of Spirit-led works because it didn't fit into how they interpreted the Mosaic Law? Indeed it was. The Pharisees didn't have sufficient knowledge to make a judgment, but they presumed to do so anyway. Jesus' response to that spirit? Woe! We don't have any room for Pharisaical prophets in the Body of Christ.

That attitude of prejudice and the act of presumption will poison a prophetic ministry. Sure, there is an antidote. It's called repentance. But why ingest the poison of presumption in the first place? Let's take a closer look at how prophets fall into presumption and how we can avoid mixing our personal prejudices into the spiritual flow.

THE ORIGIN OF OUR PROOF

First, we must be clear that there is no room for personal opinion in the prophetic. Our "proof" must come from the Holy Spirit, not our own spirits or some other spirit. As mouthpieces for God, others take our words and insights very seriously, and we cannot abuse the grace people perceive on our lives.

I learned that lesson with humility on the way to a conference in the Midwest. I was sitting in the airport with a friend, having a bite to eat as we waited for the plane to reach the gate. We were talking about various and sundry issues, including the change in European government in the wake of what some call the revived Roman Empire (the European Union).

I mentioned that the anti-Christ spirit was alive and well in the earth and speculated – I was just speculating, mind you – that the literal anti-Christ could be rising to power in this generation. Some in the end-time prophecy camp have suggested that the anti-Christ would rise up from the European Union, so the speculative conversation wasn't entirely out of left field. But it wasn't the Spirit of God showing me that, either. I was just thinking out loud. That's when the correction came.

My friend warned me to be careful not to make any presumptions. Because of the prophetic gift I carry, such discussions could sway people to believe my musings, which, again, did not come from the Spirit of God. In other words, I was just talking about possibilities, but prophets should be careful who is listening because we could cause some to stumble in what they mistakenly believe is a Spirit-inspired utterance. Prophets need to be careful with their words at all times.

What's perhaps even more dangerous than public musings is the trap of filtering prophetic utterances through our own biases. In doing so we may not only mislead the hearers, but downright deceive them. What would cause the prophet to think anyone wants his opinion, anyway? (We'll get to that in a minute.) The function of the prophet is to reveal the mind and will of God, not the mind and will of the prophet. There is a time for us to offer trusted opinions of wisdom, but it's not in the same instance as we utter "thus saith the Lord."

GOD HATES PRESUMPTION

Doubtless, God hates presumption – and He has good reason. There are several variations of the Greek word "presume." Typically, the word portrays insolence (insultingly contemptuous speech or conduct), pride, arrogance, or audacity (bold or arrogant disregard for normal restraints). Considering that the Lord includes a proud look and a false witness among the His seven abominations, presumption is not something to be taken lightly.

In fact, while the King James Version of the Bible only mentions the words presume, presumed, presumptuous and presumptuously 11 times, the act almost always leads to the death. Indeed, there are few things worse than a presumptuous prophet. Deuteronomy 18:20 declares,

> "The prophet who presumes to speak a word in my name which I have not commanded him to speak, or who speaks in the name of other gods, the same prophet shall die."

Mercy! Of course, we are living in a time of grace and even the most presumptuous prophet probably won't be struck dead for this sin. Jesus died for the sin of the world, including our occasional presumptions. But we must ask ourselves, what is happening inside of us, in our spirits, when we presume? Selah.

Look, the prophetic ministry is not an experiment in spirituality. It's not a Holy Ghost guessing game. Prophets should be statesmen. A U.S. ambassador to China would not presume to speak on behalf of the President just because a roundtable of delegates expected him to deliver some governmental wisdom. The ambassador could cause a war with his words if he speaks out of order.

Likewise, a prophet should not presume to speak on behalf of Jesus just because a congregation of priests and kings expects him to deliver some deep prophecy. The prophet can cause strife, division or other ill side effects if he presumes to speak without permission from the Spirit. The answer to presumption is the same answer Nancy Reagan offered a fifth grade girl in a California school when she asked, "What do you do if somebody offers you drugs?" Reagan told her: "Just say no."

If someone is pressuring you to prophesy, just say no. If you don't have a word, then keep your mouth shut and keep God happy. As we learned in the last chapter, it's not about pleasing man, it's about pleasing God. God hates presumption.

GRACE, YES. PRESUMPTION, NO.

Oh, but we're under a new covenant, you say? God is a God of grace. Indeed. God has always been a God of grace. But if you think God likes presumption any better in the New Testament than the Old Testament, then think again – or ask the Apostle Peter who was writing under the inspiration of the Holy Ghost when he revealed that those who walk after the flesh in the lust of uncleanness, and despise government (authority) are presumptuous, self-willed and slanderous (2 Peter 2:9-19).

After pointing out these presumptuous ones love to indulge in evil pleasures, revel in deceitfulness, possess an insatiable lust, lure people into sin, and train themselves to be greedy, among other sinful qualities, Peter finally connects them with Balaam, the presumptuous prophet.

You remember, Balaam. King Balak sent messengers to him with a sinister request and rewards of divination in their hands. Balak offered to pay Balaam to curse the Israelites. Wicked story short, Balaam initially refused to pronounce the curse, but eventually helped King Balak defile the Israelites by giving him a strategy involving sexual sin (Numbers 31:16). Balaam wound up committing treason (fighting against the Israelites) and his end was death. Listen to how the Apostle Peter referred to Balaam's presumption.

> "They have wandered off the right road and followed the way of Balaam, son of Beor, who loved to earn money by doing wrong. But Balaam was stopped from his mad course when his donkey rebuked him with a human voice. These people [Which people? Presumptuous people!] are as useless as dried-up springs of water or as clouds blown away by the wind – promising much and delivering nothing. They are doomed to blackest darkness" (2 Peter 2:15-17 MSG).

THE MINISTRY OF A CHRONICLER

Now, let's get back to our friends young Stanley and Dr. Livingstone? When I read this historical account it really hit home with me because in the secular world I've served as a journalist. (It's funny how the Lord will sometimes train you in Babylon for His Kingdom exploits. Part of my calling in the Body of

Christ is one of a chronicler. But that's another lesson for another book.)

Even by journalistic standards, Stanley would have missed it in his presumption. See, the journalist never assumes or presumes. He presses in for facts, figures and verifiable details that tell who, what, where, when, why and how – often called "the five Ws and H" in the media world – something has happened. If he makes assumptions and presumptions, he's liable to have to run a correction in the next day's paper – because he was wrong. If he keeps making those same mistakes, the editor will eventually fire him and his reputation in the media industry will go to pot. Who wants to hire a journalist who isn't accurate in their reporting – or who makes stuff up? No respectable editor that I know.

Can you see the spiritual parallel? The prophet should never presume. He should press in for truth that offers details about those five Ws and the H about something that is going to happen or something that is currently happening. If the prophet makes assumptions and presumptions, he's liable to God. He may be able to repent to the person or group that heard the presumptuous prophecy, but some level of damage is done and oftentimes healing must take place.

If the prophet keeps making the same mistake over and over again, his reputation in prophetic circles will go to pot. Not only that, it puts a blemish on the prophetic ministry as a whole. Who wants to receive a prophetic word from a prophet who is not accurate, or who presumes to speak out of order? No discerning Christian I know.

Dr. Livingstone, a now legendary missionary, penned fascinating books that sold in huge numbers all over the world as he pursued his dream to open the continent to make a way for other missionaries to preach the Gospel. Stanley, on the other hand, was notorious for changing the facts to suit his purposes – or even making them up – in his books. Stanley even lied about his heritage. He fought for the South in the American civil war, and then committed treason (just like Balaam did) and served the North when captured. He later helped the King of Belgium fulfill his greedy purposes (just like Balaam did) in Africa. Just like Balaam, Stanley's greed and pride caused him to compromise his professional ethics.

Stanley eventually became a mass murderer of Africans in the Congo region.

It seems the fate of the presumptuous is ultimately the same throughout history. Let's just take a quick look at the 11 instances in the King James translation of the Bible that deal directly with presumption and its root.

THE ISRAELITES WERE PRESUMPTUOUS

The first instance of presumption recorded in the Bible occurred after the 10 Israelites spies brought back and evil report. The people did not want to take possession of the Promised Land because giants occupied it. After they mourned at the Lord's response – He said that generation would die in the wilderness instead of seeing His best for them – they repented and decided they were well able to take the land after all. But it was too late. Their disobedience and unbelief had already tainted them.

God requires quick obedience. Many times delayed obedience will get us into grave trouble. I remember a time when it took me a while to catch on to God's will. I was dead set against completing a certain project because it was overwhelming and I was convinced that it wasn't God's timing. I was wrong. Before it was too late, He told me to finish the task. I still couldn't see it – and I didn't want to. By the time I got my heart in line with His command, it was too late. The appointed time had passed and when I did try to enter in and finish the task, it made an even bigger mess.

Ultimately, it all worked out but not without pain and heartache for me and also for those around me.

Through that experience I learned the power of quick obedience and the consequences of slow obedience. The Israelites were guilty of slow obedience, which is really just a nice way of saying "disobedience" when you get real about it. What was worse, the Israelites were being doubly disobedient because not only did they fail to believe His word, but they disobeyed Moses when he said,

> "Go not up, for the Lord is not among you; that ye be not smitten before your enemies. For the Amalekites and the Canaanites are there before you, and ye shall fall by the sword: because ye are turned away from the Lord, therefore the Lord will not be with you. But they presumed to go up unto the hill top: nevertheless the ark of the covenant of the Lord, and Moses, departed not out of the camp. Then the Amalekites came down, and the Canaanites which dwelt in that hill, and smote them, and discomfited them, even unto Hormah" (Numbers 14:42-45).

In Deuteronomy, Moses recounts the ugly scene when he said, "So I spake to you; and ye would not hear, but rebelled against the commandment of the

Lord, and went presumptuously up into the hill. And the Amorites, which dwelt in that mountain, came out against you, and chased you, as bees do, and destroyed you in Seir, even unto Hormah" (Deuteronomy 1:42-44).

As you can read, the end of presumptuous was not pretty: destruction.

PRESUMPTUOUS HAMAN

The wicked Haman presumed. Haman plotted to destroy the Israelites and, to his dismay and demise, Queen Esther found out about it. After overcoming her own fears and calling a fast among the Jews, she requested a banquet where both the king of Persia, which was her husband, and Haman would be present.

At this delectable banquet, Esther explained to the king that someone had a plan to destroy her and her people. Then the king asked her a question, "Who is he, and where is he, that durst presume in his heart to do so?" (Esther 7:5) Esther told the king it was none other than wicked Haman. The king was enraged and ordered Haman hung on the gallows he had arranged for Esther's uncle, Mordecai. Once again, the end of presumption was not pretty: death.

PRESUMPTUOUSLY
UNDER THE LAW

Again, we are in a time of grace. God is not waiting to send a lightning bolt if we fall into this trap, (but that doesn't mean we shouldn't attempt to avoid it.) Even in the Old Testament, God looked one way at acts that are unintentional and another way at acts that are presumptuous. This is clearly illustrated in the Law.

> "Ye shall have one law for him that sinneth through ignorance, both for him that is born among the children of Israel, and for the stranger that sojourneth among them. But the soul that doeth ought presumptuously, whether he be born in the land, or a stranger, the same reproacheth the Lord; and that soul shall be cut off from among his people. Because he hath despised the word of the Lord, and hath broken his commandment, that soul shall utterly be cut off; his iniquity shall be upon him" (Numbers 15:29-31).

Being "cut off" may sound harsh, but it only serves to illustrate how God feels about presumption. Here's a good example of why the Lord will make an example out of certain people who act presumptuous – for the greater good. The death sentence God imposed on presumption was to save many others from committing the same sin:

> "And the man that will do presumptuously, and will not hearken unto the priest that standeth to minister there before the Lord thy God, or unto the judge, even that man shall die: and thou shalt put away the evil from Israel And all the people shall hear, and fear, and do no more presumptuously" (Deuteronomy 17:12-13).

> "If a man come presumptuously upon his neighbor, to slay him with guile; thou shalt take him from mine altar, that he may die" (Exodus 21:14).

PROPHETS WERE PRESUMPTUOUS

Now let's bring it a little closer to home by taking a look at presumptuous prophets in the Old Testament. Here are two examples from Deuteronomy.

"But a prophet who presumes to speak in my name anything I have not commanded him to say, or a prophet who speaks in the name of other gods, must be put to death" (Deuteronomy 18:20).

"When a prophet speaketh in the name of the Lord, if the thing follow not, nor come to pass, that is the thing which the Lord hath not spoken, but the prophet hath spoken it presumptuously: thou shalt not be afraid of him" (Deuteronomy 18:22).

NEW TESTAMENT PRESUMPTION

Can we bring it even closer to home? How about right in your living room – the New Testament. Again, Peter had plenty to say about presumption; none of it good.

"But chiefly them that walk after the flesh in the lust of uncleanness, and despise government. Presumptuous are they, selfwilled, they are not afraid to speak evil of dignities" (2 Peter 2:10).

The only time in the Bible where presumption has a positive connotation is in one of David's prayers. In

Psalm 19:13 he cried, "Keep back thy servant also from presumptuous sins; let them not have dominion over me: then I shall be upright, and I shall be innocent from the great transgression." Thank God we have a Savior. We can repent of such sinful works. We need to pray like David.

AVOIDING PRESUMPTION

Let's not forget the secondary meaning of presumption: to overstep one's bounds. Prophets must recognize boundaries and not take the liberty of overstepping prophetic authority. Yes, where the Spirit of the Lord is there is liberty, but not liberty to speak outside God-given spiritual jurisdiction. That jurisdiction begins in the local church and expands as the prophet matures. Even the President of the United States, with all his authority, would be presumptuous to issue a decree over another nation. His words would fall to the ground because he would be overstepping his bounds.

You can avoid presumption by refusing to prophesy without an unction. An unction could be described as a green light from the Holy Spirit to prophesy. You may feel a bubbling forth in your spirit that compels you to speak. As you mature in the prophetic, it will become easier to recognize that unction.

Here's a practical tip: If you believe the Lord is speaking to you, but you are not entirely sure, then preface your utterance with "I believe the Lord is saying." Here's another practical tip: When you believe the Lord is speaking to you, be it through an impression, a vision, a word coming unto you saying, etc., make a record of how He spoke to you, what He said, and whether it came to pass. If you continually conclude you are accurate with dreams and visions but less accurate with hearing and impressions, then that knowledge will offer you confidence in the precision of your dreams and visions and help you proceed with caution on hearing and impressions.

Finally, if you've missed it, if you've presumed, if you've stepped out of line, then simply repent. But don't just say "I'm sorry, God" and move on to the next prophetic word. Ask the Lord how you missed it. Was it pride that caused you to speak out of turn? Was it innocent zeal gone wild? Was it a hurt, wound, headache, or spicy food-induced dream? We don't grow in the prophetic by taking the word of the Lord lightly. When we make a mistake, we need to find out why and make it right, if possible, and then get back on the humble horse and continue on.

PROPHETIC KEYS

+ When you presume you form an opinion from little or no evidence. Presumption also means to take as true or as fact without actual proof. Presumptuous could also mean "to overstep due bounds" and "to take liberties."

+ First, we must be clear that there is no room for personal opinion in the prophetic. Our "proof" must come from the Holy Spirit, not our own spirits or some other spirit. As mouthpieces for God, others take our words and insights very seriously, and we cannot abuse the grace people perceive on our lives.

+ A prophet should not presume to speak on behalf of Jesus just because a congregation of priests and kings expects him to deliver some deep prophecy. The prophet can cause strife, division or other ill side effects if he presumes to speak without permission from the Spirit.

+ If the prophet keeps making the same mistake over and over again, his reputation in prophetic circles will go to pot. Not only that, it puts a blemish on the prophetic ministry as a whole.

+ You can avoid presumption by refusing to prophesy without an unction. An unction could be described as a green light from the Holy Spirit to prophesy. You may feel a bubbling forth in your spirit that compels you to speak.

+ Ask the Lord how you missed it. Was it pride that caused you to speak out of turn? Was it innocent zeal gone wild? Was it a hurt, wound, headache, or spicy food-induced dream? We don't grow in the prophetic by taking the word of the Lord lightly.

Chapter 6

THE SELF-WILLED
PROPHET

Many will say to me in that day, Lord, Lord, have we not prophesied in thy name? and in thy name cast out devils? and in thy name done many wonderful works? And I will profess unto them, I never knew you: depart from me, ye that work iniquity (Matthew 7:22-23).

The Holy Spirit is a practical Teacher. He doesn't always choose to send an angel or a prophet to declare His will for our lives, nor does He always speak to us in a still, small voice. No, sometimes the Lord sends loud and clear messages through our natural surroundings. It is up to us to remain sensitive enough to the Spirit to see prophetic implications in every day life.

Indeed, remaining sensitive to the Holy Spirit offers us the ultimate navigational system. You'll never wind up taking a dangerous detour off the prophetic highway if you stay tuned to your supernatural Global Positioning Satellite (GPS) system. It's more accurate than any 21st century technology and it never fails to show you where you need to go and exactly how to get there, albeit often one faith-filled step at a time. You just have to remember to flip the switch, so to speak as you set your mind on the things of the Spirit instead of on the things of the flesh.

I'm accustomed to the Holy Ghost speaking to me through the illumination of natural events that correspond to spiritual truths. Don't get me wrong. I don't look for deep prophetic directives if I lose a button on my blouse. (You can get goofy in a hurry if you try to tie the voice of God to anything and everything). But I do try to remain aware of the Holy Spirit's presence and ask Him if there is significance to people, places or objects that strike my spirit. I'm sure you do the same.

GIVE ME A SIGN!?

Like the time I was driving down Interstate 95 coming into Ft. Lauderdale. I saw a row of orange garage-like doors that I had seen many times before in passing. This time, the colors seemed bolder, more vibrant, almost glowing. I don't remember the brand name of the facility, but I do remember two key words on that sign: Self Storage. I continued to drive down the highway with an "hmm" floating around in my soul. Suddenly, a sign above a row of blue doors with those same two words – self storage – demanded my attention.

"OK, God. What's up?" I asked, certain I was about to miss an important lesson if I failed to inquire at His temple. Well, it doesn't take a prophet to interpret the message. It was clearer than 20/20 vision: It was time to put my "self" in storage. It was time to decrease a little more that He might increase. It was time to exchange the heavy weight of self-will for self-sacrifice. It was time to go to a new level.

Maybe you've been there. You are frustrated because you know the prophetic gift of God inside you should be producing more. After all, you've read the books, you've gone to the prayer meetings, and you've even plugged in to the work of the ministry. Yet you feel more like a stagnant reservoir than a free-flowing river. Of course, there could be many different reasons why your breakthrough hasn't manifested. But will you, just for a moment, entertain the notion that it could have something to do with your "self"?

There is something I call the self-willed syndrome that I can share with you for a good reason: I've lived with it and learned to recognize its onset. While we all have our own will, we have a choice of how we will use it. When we align ourselves with God's will, all is well with us. It's only when we start trumpeting the "what about me?" song that a potentially deadly group of signs and symptoms reveals this sickly spiritual condition.

What we're about to find out is that self can both hold you back from breakthrough and hold you back from entering the Kingdom of God.

SELF THIS, SELF THAT AND SELF THE OTHER

Webster's dictionary has a laundry list of definitions that begin with "self." Most of them are self-serving. There's self-absorption, self-advancement, self-appointed. And we haven't even got out of the As yet. There's self-deception, self-existent and self-government. There's self-indulgence, self-justification and self-reliance. Oh, let's not forget self-righteousness, that religious version that looks good on the outside but is rotten on the inside.

Get the picture? (Perhaps that's why the Lord showed me a row of doors. One self-storage unit for each of the "self" areas I needed to put away.) All that said, I believe the very worst self-issue is self-will. A self-willed person is stubborn about getting his or her own way. A self-willed person is a willful person. The willful person does what he or she pleases. The only problem is when what he or she pleases does not please God. That's when self-will takes us down the path of self-government past the alley of self-indulgence and toward the path of self-deception.

The Bible, for example, says that a bishop must not be self-willed (Titus 1:7). How much more a prophet who is supposed to be a mouthpiece of God? The prophet must serve the will of God at all costs. It doesn't always make sense to our souls, but it's not our job to figure out God's grand plan. It's our job to help fulfill it.

Hosea tells the story of Ephraim, which "played the prostitute." Hosea explains, "Ephraim is oppressed, crushed in judgment, because in selfwill he walked after the commandment of man" (Hosea 5:11 DBY). And the Apostle Peter mentions a group that walks after the lusts of the flesh and describes them as self-willed (2 Peter 2:10). He calls this group "spots" and "blemishes." He says they are deceitful and will receive the wages of unrighteousness. That's not exactly the company I want to keep, but you know what they say: Birds of a feather flock together.

HAVE WE NOT PROPHESIED IN YOUR NAME?

Now let's bring this home: Self-will is one ingredient in the recipe for a false prophet. How can I say that? I don't have to. Jesus said it for me and Matthew recorded it in his Gospel. In Matthew 7:15 Jesus tells us to beware of false prophets who appear as harmless as doves but are as dangerous as serpents. Then in Verse 21 Jesus goes on to warn the disciples that not everyone who says "Lord, Lord" will enter into the Kingdom of heaven. Jesus makes it crystal clear that only those who do the will of the Father will enter in.

> "Many will say to me in that day, Lord, Lord, have we not prophesied in thy name? and in thy name cast out devils? and in thy name done

many wonderful works? And I will profess unto them, I never knew you: depart from me, ye that work iniquity" (Matthew 7:22-23).

So what are we going to do with that? Jesus undeniably calls out those who prophesy, cast out devils, and do mighty works. He is obviously talking about prophetic ministry in these verses (not that they don't apply to anyone else). Jesus began His teaching with a warning about false prophets and then drilled down to the core issue of some false prophets: self-will.

Let's look at this verse again in light of other translations of the Greek words. "Prophesied" translates as "exercised the prophetic office." "Name" translates as "authority." "Wonderful works" translates as "miracles." "Knew" translates as "allowed." And "iniquity" translates as "lawlessness." So Matthew 7:22-23 could read this way:

Many will say to me in that day, Lord, Lord, have we not exercised the prophetic office by your authority? and by your authority cast out devils? and by your authority done many miracles? And I will profess unto them, I never allowed you: depart from me, ye that work lawlessness.

In other words, "You did not do the will of My Father. You did your own will. You were self-willed. You did what you wanted to do without asking God what He thought about it. You prophesied without permission. You cast out devils to draw attention to yourself. You used your gifts, which are without repentance, as it pleased you. You may have used My name, but I didn't call you to do those things."

MAKING IT
PROPHETICALLY PLAIN

Let me hit this self-willed devil right out of the ballpark with the Message Bible translation: "I can see it now — at the Final Judgment thousands strutting up to me saying, 'Master, we preached the message, we bashed the demons, our God-sponsored projects had everyone talking.' And do you know what I am going to say? 'You missed the boat. All you did was use me to make yourselves important. You don't impress me one bit. You're out of here'" (Matthew 7:22-23).

I don't know about you, but that was enough to drive me to the self-storage facility and pay the price to rent as many units as it takes to unload self-assertion, self-conceit, self-interest — and self-will. It's a character issue. Jesus said we would know people by their fruit. But looking at the fruit of a ministry is not enough. We must look at character, which should be ever-ripening without rotting.

Think about Jesus, the Prophet. He is our prototype and it is His testimony we speak when we prophesy.

"Jesus didn't seek His own will. He sought the will of the Father who sent Him" (John 6:38).

Doubtless, being committed to the will of the Father was much easier for Him when He was casting out devils and prophesying, but He stuck to His guns even to the point of blood.

You remember the episode in the Garden of Gethsemane. The hour of His betrayal was at hand. He admitted to Peter and the two sons of Zebedee that His soul was exceedingly sorrowful – even to death. He asked God to spare Him the pain of the cross and His subsequent separation from the King of Glory three times, but each time Jesus ended His prayer with the same essential words:

"Not my will but yours be done" (Matthew 26).

PICK UP YOUR CROSS
AND FOLLOW HIM

Jesus understands it's not always easy to put down our own wills to do the will of the Father, and He has given us the power of the Holy Spirit to help us take up our cross and follow His example. I like the way the Amplified Bible puts it. Jesus just rebuked Peter, saying, "Get behind Me, Satan!" because He was trying to talk Jesus out of going to the cross. Then Jesus used it as a teaching example in Mark 8:33-36:

> "For you do not have a mind intent on promoting what God wills, but what pleases men [you are not on God's side, but that of men]. And Jesus called [to Him] the throng with His disciples and said to them, If anyone intends to come after Me, let him deny himself [forget, ignore, disown, and lose sight of himself and his own interests] and take up his cross, and [joining Me as a disciple and siding with My party] follow with Me [continually, cleaving steadfastly to Me]."

In his book "Purifying the Prophetic: Breaking Free from the Spirit of Self-Fulfillment,"[10] R. Loren

Sandford offers a sign of the times and calls for Christians to recall the Lord's words in Matthew 16, "If anyone wishes to come after me, he must deny himself, take up his cross and follow Me. For whoever wishes to save his life will lose it; but whoever loses his life for My sake will find it." With clear prophetic urgency Sandford writes:

> "Self-focus is killing us. We are losing our lives, but for all the wrong reasons – not for the Lord's sake, but for pursuit of self. Self-absorption has become so much a part of our culture, and we have become so accustomed to it, that it has come to feel completely natural to us. We fail to see how deeply we have been captivated by it and have become unaware of how much we have lost."

Kingdom prophets and prophetic people, maybe you are like me and have seen the same self-storage sign. I challenge you not to flow in spiritual gifts without exercising self-control, self-denial and self-discipline. I appeal to you to go through some self-examination, self-restraint and self-revealing. Rid yourself of self-will. Self-will is stubbornness. Stubbornness is as iniquity and idolatry (1 Samuel 15:23). The road to self-deception is not as long as you might think. And the end is self-destruction. Let's continually visit the self-storage facility and offload all that is unpleasing to God so that we can give our entire will to the Lord Almighty.

PROPHETIC KEYS

+ There is something I call the self-willed syndrome that I can share with you for a good reason: I've lived with it and learned to recognize its onset. While we all have our own will, we have a choice of how we will use it. When we align ourselves with God's will, all is well with us.

+ The Bible says that a bishop must not be self-willed (Titus 1:7). How much more a prophet who is supposed to be a mouthpiece of God? The prophet must serve the will of God at all costs.

+ Think about Jesus, the Prophet. He is our prototype Prophet and it is His testimony we speak when we prophesy. Jesus sought not His own will, but the will of the Father who sent Him (John 6:38).

+ It's a character issue. Jesus said we would know people by their fruit. But looking at the fruit of a ministry is not enough. We must look at character, which should be ever-ripening without rotting.

+ Kingdom prophets and prophetic people, maybe you are like me and have seen the same self-storage sign. I challenge you not to flow in spiritual gifts without exercising self-control, self-denial and self-discipline. I appeal to you to go through some self-examination, self-restraint and self-revealing.

Chapter 7

JEZEBEL'S CONTROLLING PROPHETS

Notwithstanding I have a few things against thee, because thou sufferest that woman Jezebel, which calleth herself a prophetess, to teach and to seduce my servants to commit fornication, and to eat things sacrificed unto idols (Revelation 2:20).

Have you ever noticed prophecy draws an audience? People will stand in a prayer line for hours to receive a prophetic word. And it seems everybody wants to be friends with the prophetic intercessor. That's because people are searching for purpose, identity, and direction in their lives and they know that prophetic announcements can help them come into another dimension of their destiny – and prophets are channels through which God speaks.

With prophetic grace comes influence. If a prophet has a track record for accuracy, his gift can bring him before great men. But revelations – the secrets God shares with His servants the prophets – can become a temptation for anyone who is not walking in love. It was the Apostle Paul who said,

"Mere knowledge causes people to be puffed up (to bear themselves loftily and be proud), but love (affection, goodwill and benevolence) edifies and builds up and encourages one to grow [to his full stature]" (1 Corinthians 8:1 AMP).

That sort of sounds like part of the mandate of five-fold prophets, doesn't it? The Apostle Paul said something similar about the purpose of five-fold ascension gifts – apostles, prophets, evangelists, pastors and teachers – that Christ gave to the Church:

"His intention was the perfecting and the full equipping of the saints (His consecrated people), [that they should do] the work of ministering toward building up Christ's body (the church) [That it might develop] until we all attain oneness in the faith and in the comprehension of the [full and accurate] knowledge of the Son of God, that [we might arrive] at really mature manhood (the completeness of personality which is nothing less than the standard height of Christ's own perfection), the measure of the stature of the fullness of the Christ and the completeness found in Him" (Ephesians 4:12-13).

THE KING OF LOVE

Let's take a little bunny trail now for a closer look at what love really is – and what it is not. The Apostle Paul said even though he had the gift of prophecy and understood all mysteries and all knowledge, and had faith enough to move mountains, and gave away all he had to feed the poor and offered himself as a martyr, it wouldn't mean anything without love. And here's his Holy Ghost-inspired definition of love:

"Charity suffereth long, and is kind; charity envieth not; charity vaunteth not itself, is not puffed up, Doth not behave itself unseemly, seeketh not her own, is not easily provoked, thinketh no evil; Rejoiceth not in iniquity, but rejoiceth in the truth; Beareth all things, believeth all things, hopeth all things, endureth all things. Charity never faileth: but whether there be prophecies, they shall fail; whether there be tongues, they shall cease; whether there be knowledge, it shall vanish away" (1 Corinthians 13:4-8).

I have a lot to say about these verses in connection with prophetic ministry, but for the purposes of this book I just want to point out one thing: Control is not one of the characteristics of love. The Holy Ghost doesn't control us. He is a gentleman. It grieves Him when misguided prophets use the influence afforded them as a mouthpiece of God to deliver adulterated prophetic words, curses, or other controlling or fearful utterances.

Let's take it one step further. What is the purpose of prophecy? Well, the Apostle Paul cites three of them: to edify, comfort and exhort (1 Corinthians 14:3). The Amplified Bible translates the verse this way... "upbuilding and constructive spiritual progress and encouragement and consolation." And The Message has this to say, "so that they can grow and be strong and experience His presence with you." Hmm. No control there. Yes, the ministry of the prophet carries an anointing to guide, correct and on rare occasions even utter true correction of the Spirit. Still, that doesn't account for control.

THE QUEEN OF CONTROL

Now bear with me for a moment while we compare love, edification, comfort and exhortation to control, one of the devil's ways of perverting the purpose of prophetic ministry. To control is to exercise restraining or directing influence over, or to have power over another person. Prophets need to exercise self-control through the power of the Holy Ghost, but have no business seeking to control anyone else. Yet, I've seen a few too many prophets' ministries sidetracked by this spirit, which is commonly called Jezebel.

Jezebel gained her reputation as an enemy to the prophets of God in the Old Testament era. While dogs devoured the wicked Queen Jezebel, make no mistake, her spirit is alive in New Testament times. Indeed, Queen Jezebel is infamous for her antics in the Book of I Kings. Jezebel is charged with murdering many prophets and cutting off the voices of others that fearfully hid in caves (1 Kings 18:4, 13). The Book of Revelation exposes this spirit's operation in the New Testament age as one that "calls herself a prophetess," to teach and seduce the Lord's true prophets with lust and idolatry (Revelation 2:20).

JEZEBEL'S REVENGE ON ELIJAH

The spirit of Jezebel is still targeting the spirit of Elijah. In other words, the false prophetic, controlling, manipulative spirit is on the hunt for those who carry the prophetic mantel. Queen Jezebel failed miserably in her attempt to kill the Prophet Elijah. Yes, he took the bait of fear and ran into a cave, but he remerged and went on to anoint others who would thwart the agenda of the wicked queen and ultimately take her out. That spirit, though, did not die. The spirit that was influencing Queen Jezebel, the spirit of control that we refer to as a Jezebel spirit today, never stopped pursuing those who walk in the spirit and power of Elijah.

In fact, in the New Testament we see that the spirit of Jezebel got a measure of revenge on the spirit of Elijah, at least temporally. You remember the scene.

It was Herod's birthday. Herodias' daughter, Salome, danced for Herod and his guests. He enjoyed it so much he promised with an oath to give her whatever she asked, up to half his kingdom (Matthew 14:6). Salome turned to her mother for advice about what to request. I can just see it now. The Jezebel spirit that influenced Herodias whispered, "This is your chance! You can silence that voice that's been exposing your sin. Ask for John the Baptist's head!" And so it was. Herod, though grieved, kept his oath. John met with the gallows and Salome delivered the prophet's head to her mother on a silver platter. We know the spirit of Elijah that rested on John was unharmed, but John could no longer carry that fiery, reforming prophetic mantle. Jezebel got a measure of revenge.

While Jezebel has not given up on her mission to cut off the prophetic voice, God's mouthpieces are no longer ignorant to her devices. This powerful principality is now employing more subtle tactics in effort to corrupt the reformation. Yes, Jezebel continues to war against prophets, intercessors and whomever else is carrying the voice of God. Of course, Jezebel's preference is to use you as a vessel or a eunuch. She wants to flow through you to do her dirty work. If she can't flow through you, though, she'll try to take your head as a trophy. Either way, Jezebel has carved out a monumental pothole that will not only hinder your accuracy, it will also lead you into divination.

JEZEBEL'S SEDUCTION

Jezebel targets those who are rebellious, weak or wounded and she knows how to use deep hurts and wounds to mislead and exploit. But, as Apostle Jonas Clark points out in his best-selling Christian classic, "Jezebel: Seducing Goddess of War," Jezebel has to seduce you before she can use you. To seduce means to lure, entice, tempt, or beguile, in an effort to mislead. The prophet who is flowing in a spirit of Jezebel will exercise prophetic control. Let's see what Apostle Clark wrote about Jezebel in his book [11]:

> "Remember that both Jezebels mentioned in Scripture were false prophetesses. The spirit of Jezebel views personal prophecy as a manipulative means to an ungodly end. Some personal prophecy in the Church today is nothing more than Jezebel's controlling spiritual utterances."

Apostle Clark is an expert on the spirit of Jezebel and I would recommend that you pick up his book on the topic for an in-depth look at the workings of this spirit. My focus in this chapter is to demonstrate how prophets and intercessors can fall prey to this spirit, which destroys ministries. How does Jezebel win prophets to her dinner table? Again, the seduction must come first.

Remember when Ahab was depressed because he wanted Naboth's vineyard. In summary, Jezebel said, "Don't worry about it. I'll get it for you." You see, Jezebel didn't take the kingdom away from Ahab – Ahab gave her his authority. What's in you that would allow Jezebel to undermine your authority as a prophet or intercessor? What do her wiles tap into in you? Selah. Pause and think about that for a moment.

OPENING THE DOOR TO JEZEBEL

If we all recognized the spirit of control for what it was, we'd slam the door in its face when it came knocking. Unfortunately, we sometimes have to slam the door on some character flaws before we can shut out the possibility of tapping into control. There are three areas I want to focus on for the purposes of this book: rebellion, hurts and wounds, and rejection.

Let's start with rebellion. The Bible says rebellion is as the sin of witchcraft (1 Samuel 15:23). The Bible discusses Jezebel and her witchcrafts (2 Kings 9:22). We know that Jezebel didn't submit to the authority of her husband, Ahab, rather she sought opportunity to usurp it. What about you? Are you submitted to your husband, the set-man of your local church, and other authorities God has placed in your life? Of course, rebellion opens the door to all sorts of sin, flowing in control is merely one of them.

It's been said that submission is an attitude of the heart. But rebellion is also an attitude of the heart, and one that manifests in subtle ways despite surface-level submission. Surely, if you've made it this deep into the book you are not in full-blown rebellion. You are seeking to refine your character so you can make less room for the flesh and more room for Jesus. But what about subtle rebellious attitudes and mindsets? How do you respond when someone tells you, "no." If you get your back up, the spirit of control may be influencing you. The word "no" tends to make the Jezebel spirit manifest.

What about those areas of our emotions, reasoning and imaginations you don't talk about with anyone?

You know in your heart of hearts your attitudes are wrong, but your feelings won't line up with what you know is right. So you hold on to the subtleties of rebellion. A small crack in the dam can lead to disaster. If you ask the Lord, He will show you any attitudes that are not Christ-like and if you are willing to change He will offer you His perspective and you will begin to see submission as a safety net rather than bondage.

MAKING A COVENANT
WITH JEZEBEL

Jezebel takes advantage of us while we are down. I remember a time when I felt as if I had been taken advantage of and was extremely hurt. I was indeed a wounded soldier. In fact, I was lying in my bed in the middle of the afternoon wallowing in self-pity and licking those wounds. What I discovered was that hurts and wounds are bitter. If you do not allow the Lord to heal them, you will develop a root of bitterness that will spring forth and defile your prophetic flow.

So anyway, there I was in the midst of my pity party when I heard the voice of Jezebel. This spirit of control came whispering, "You can't let anything like this ever happen again. You'd better guard yourself or they'll hurt you again. You are in control." Because I had been trained well in an apostolic ministry – by the very one who 'wrote the book' on Jezebel – I recognized this as Jezebel attempting to cajole me into making a covenant with the spirit of control that would "protect me" from getting hurt again. Of course, making that covenant – agreeing with that voice – would have been sort of like Ahab handing his authority over to Jezebel. That spirit would have influenced me in all of my relationships.

Thank God He opened my eyes to Jezebel's assignment. I rose up and said, "No!" The voice woke me from my pitiful slumber and caused me to rise up and cry to the Lord to take away the hurt and heal the wound. I forgave those who had hurt me and prayed for God to bless them. When I submitted myself to God and resisted the devil, that wicked spirit fled from me (James 4:7). I shudder to think how my soul would have filtered life's events if I had succumbed to the devil's wiles as Ahab did.

Maybe you have taken on the attitude that promises, "No one will ever hurt me again." If you have, then you've opened yourself up for a spirit to fortify your stance and pervert your responses to the people around you. If this is allowed to go on unchecked, it could cause you to put up walls around you so that even the very truth of God's Word would have a hard time getting in. If truth isn't going in, then I submit to you that truth isn't coming out.

You can't prophesy accurately in this condition. If pain is hidden in the recesses of your soul, buried from the Holy Spirit's probe, then that pain could come out in the form of adulterated prophecies. If you want to rise to greater level of accuracy, ask the Holy Spirit to heal you of every old wound and pray for those who have spitefully used you (Matthew 5:44).

INSECURITIES, REJECTIONS AND HIDDEN FEARS

Some other playgrounds for Jezebel are insecurities, rejection and hidden fears. Since everybody is insecure about something, no one is immune to Jezebel. Jezebel probes your soul to discover your insecurities and hidden fears so she can exploit them later. Flattery works well on folks who have insecurities and hidden fears or rejection. Jezebel can smooth talk them. Jezebel can tell them how great a singer they are or how powerful a preacher they are. Whether it's true or not, they'll receive it because they want to. It makes them feel better about their insecure selves. Then Jezebel can manipulate and tap into their pride. Jezebel will tell them how they should be elevated to a more visible position in the ministry. Jezebel will tell them how their gift should be making more room for them.

I'll share more about that in a moment. Suffice it to say Jezebel will seek to control you by petting insecurities and alleviating your hidden fears. What are you insecure about? What are you afraid of? Our confidence should be in Christ in us. He hasn't given us a spirit of fear, but of power, love and a sound mind (2 Timothy 1:7). It may seem like a pedestrian Scripture, but if we really had a revelation of that I believe the Body of Christ would rise up and take dominion rather than lying down in timidity and watching sinners eat the good of the land. Prophets need to get this so they can herald it, but so long as prophets are bound up with rejection, Jezebel will get the best of them.

One of my prophetic mentors has said, "You can't have a prophet full of rejection." Why is that? Because it opens the door for Jezebel. Jezebel targets hurts and wounds and, unfortunately, many prophets have a root of rejection. It may be that you were different, even from your childhood years. It may be that the local church doesn't understand your gift and has rejected you along with God's voice. Rejection comes through many channels, and it's poison for the prophet because it opens the door to control, fear of man, fear of failure, and a host of other ungodly emotions. In his book, "Life After Rejection"[12] Apostle Jonas Clark writes, "A person with rejection who refuses to submit to the rule of God will lose the liberty that he takes for granted and exchange it for the control and lordship of another." Prophets must get free from rejection – continually examining their hearts for traces of this spiritual disease – so we don't find ourselves eating at Jezebel's dinner table with a company of false prophets.

GUARDING FROM JEZEBEL

Throughout this chapter we've discussed ways to guard your heart from the spirit of control that pollutes the prophetic flow. Now I want to remind you that Ahab gave his authority to Jezebel. Jezebel can't just take our authority. We have to give it to her. Ignorance to the truth that we have authority or ignorance of submission to authority is harmful to prophets.

You give Jezebel your authority any time you won't stand in your role. Whenever God tells you to do something and you don't do it, you give up your authority to this controlling, manipulative spirit. For example, when the Apostle says he needs an intercessor to head up a prayer team and you don't step into your role, you are late, you don't take the responsibility fully, Jezebel will surely volunteer. When he says he needs you to teach Kid's Church and you think you are too busy or too good for it, Jezebel volunteers in your place. It seems Jezebel is always available.

People flowing in the spirit of Jezebel find the needs of the leader in the local church and volunteer to fill the gap. They are not pure, but they are willing to do the job. So when you disobey God, Jezebel gets in your place. What am I saying? I'm telling you that merely rebuking Jezebel isn't going to stop her. You can't pray and fast Jezebel away. You only stop this spirit's operation in your life when you obey God's will. Getting in your place in God is one way to dismantle her. But she won't stop there. Even when you get in your role, she'll still try to usurp your authority.

SUBMISSION AND AUTHORITY

I'd be negligent not to remind you of the need for prophets and intercessors to submit to spiritual authority. Some prophets mistakenly think they don't need to submit to anyone, but the Bible clearly states that we are to submit ourselves one to another in the fear of God (Ephesians 5:21).

If we are islands unto ourselves, enjoying the tropical vacation, we are likely to discover that we are actually shipwrecked and in need of a rescue mission. Of course, and this also bears repeating, the Bible says submit yourself to God, resist the devil and he will flee. Listen, you can bind and loose all you want. If you are not submitted to God then it won't do you any good. If you are acting like the devil, then you can't take authority over the devil.

How does submission to authority guard you from Jezebel? It guards us because sometimes we can't see the truth. Jezebel, a false prophetess, uses her witchcrafts and witchcrafts often work in the realm of imagination. Jezebel uses imaginations to set up vain mental images strategically designed to propel you away from the Spirit's plan for your life. Spoken by the mouth of a prophet, vain imaginations have controlling power. Find some leaders you can trust and allow them to speak into your life, to be an extra set of eyes when yours are clouded with Jezebel's witchcrafts.

What's more, stay plugged in with stable Christians (Hebrews 10:25). The Bible says don't forsake the assembling of yourselves together. Don't isolate yourself. Jezebel thrives on isolated prophets because she has you all to herself. She can bombard you with every wicked imagination and watch you wallow in self-pity. I speak from experience. Find some fellow soldiers to pray with you and break that power off your mind. Soon, you'll see for yourself and be ye thankful when you do.

WALKING IN HUMILITY

Submission to authority requires humility. Humility also guards you from Jezebel's flattery. Like submission, humility is not an act. It's an attitude of the heart. Your attitude should be the same as Christ Jesus'. He knew His authority and position, but He did not consider equality with God something to be grasped.

> "He made Himself nothing, taking the very nature of a servant, being made in human likeness. And being found in the appearance as a man, he humbled himself and became obedient to death – even death on a cross!" (Philippians 2:5-8 NIV)

Thank God you don't have to die on a cross for the sin of the world. But you will have to crucify your sinful flesh – every day. Pride is not something we get totally delivered from. It's in our carnal nature. It's a constant war within ourselves, but with the help of the Holy Ghost we can walk in humility.

Here's a strategy: Know who you are in Christ – and who you are not. And don't try to be something God has not called you to be. Don't compare yourself to others because one of two things is bound to happen: You'll either feel inferior and get down on yourself or you'll feel superior and begin to walk in pride. Soon enough, you'll stumble over your inflated ego. Listen, my Apostle always says, "I don't want my gift to take me somewhere my character can't keep me." I agree wholeheartedly. If you humble yourself, God will exalt you in due time (1 Peter 5:6). It's the due time that impatient prophets don't want to hear about. Impatience is an earmark of pride, and the Bible tells us that God resists the proud and gives grace to the humble (1 Peter 5:5).

THE KEY
TO CONQUERING JEZEBEL

Now that you've submitted yourself to God, examined your heart and experienced God's cleansing fire, there is still one more task to accomplish. There is one more key to conquering Jezebel and the spirit of control she will try to inject into your ministry. See, once you submit, stand and walk in humility, Jezebel will attack in a different way. She'll try to stop you dead in your tracks.

The good news is when you know your authority and you are submitted to a godly authority (a false prophet submitted to a false apostle doesn't count) you can rise up in the spirit of Jehu the Conqueror and defeat the Jezebel spirit. Jehu received a divine commission from God to smite the house of Ahab and he was successful in doing so (2 Kings 9-10). You have also received a commission of God to put Christ's enemies under your feet (Psalm 110:1). Don't tolerate Jezebel. Jesus wouldn't and He doesn't want you to either (Revelation 2:20).

We are also called to conquer the enemy. We have to run to the battle line with a militant determination. It takes ruthless faith and militant determination to defeat Jezebel. When you sense Jezebel's attack — run to the battle. Don't withdrawal into your cave. You've got to learn how to recognize the onslaught. She uses imaginations, confusion, fear and witchcraft. You've got to be on the offense, not the defense. Be a doer of the

Word. Have a bold pursuit of the Lord. Pray fervently. Pray in tongues. Plead the blood of Jesus. Exercise your spiritual authority.

The devil has already been defeated. Jezebel's fate is sealed. Jesus promises to throw her on a bed of anguish, bring down pressing distress and severe affliction, and strike her proper followers dead (Revelation 2:22-23 AMP). But if you want authority over the nations you first have to stand in authority over Jezebel. The warfare might seem too much, but remember the reward for those who overcome:

> "He that overcometh, and keepeth my works unto the end, to him will I give power over the nations...." (Revelation 2:26).

PROPHETIC KEYS

+ Jezebel gained her reputation as an enemy to the prophets of God in the Old Testament era. While dogs devoured the wicked Queen Jezebel, make no mistake, her spirit is alive in New Testament times.

+ The spirit of Jezebel is still targeting the spirit of Elijah. In other words, the false prophetic, controlling, manipulative spirit is on the hunt for those who carry the prophetic mantel.

+ Jezebel targets those who are rebellious, weak or wounded and she knows how to use deep hurts and wounds to mislead and exploit.

+ Maybe you have taken on the attitude that promises, "No one will ever hurt me again." If you have, then you've opened yourself up for a spirit to fortify your stance and pervert your responses to the people around you.

+ Some of Jezebel's playgrounds are insecurity, rejection and hidden fears. Since everybody is insecure about something, no one is immune to Jezebel. Jezebel probes your soul to discover your insecurities and hidden fears so that she can exploit them later.

+ Some prophets mistakenly think they don't need to submit to anyone, but the Bible clearly states that we are to submit ourselves one to another in the fear of God (Ephesians 5:21).

✦ It takes ruthless faith and militant determination to defeat Jezebel. When you sense Jezebel's attack – run to the battle. Don't withdrawal into your cave. You've got to learn how to recognize the onslaught.

Chapter 8

THE GREEDY
PROPHET

Guard yourselves and keep free from all covetousness (the immoderate desire for wealth, the greedy longing to have more); for a man's life does not consist in and is not derived from possessing overflowing abundance or that which is over and above his needs (Isaiah 56:10-11 AMP).

L ike a flawed diamond that is not worth its karat weight, there are many sides to error. Resisting prideful tendencies can be a constant battle for prophets because knowledge puffeth up (1 Corinthians 8:1). As revelatory gifts to the Body of Christ, pride often tries to tempt the prophetic minister so God will have little choice but to sit him on the humbling bench for a game or two – or even an entire season. So far as lust, well, we've seen far too many men of God fall to the lust of the flesh – sexual sin that devastated those close to them and brought a reproach on the prophetic ministry.

There is yet another lust – the lust of the eyes – that I believe every rising prophet will have to face down. The lust of the eyes is really nothing more than greed. Greed is selfish and excessive desire for more of something – oftentimes money – than is needed. Yes, God is a God of more than enough and we should want more than enough so we can help others who don't have enough. We should want to be blessed in abundance so we can be an abundant blessing. That's not greed. Greed is when you want more than you need because you are just plain selfish. Greed wants to keep up with the Joneses. Greed may also be a manifestation of distrust in God as your provider. In any case, the greedy prophet wants to horde cash to himself to supply all his needs according to his own deceitful riches in vain glory.

BLIND, IGNORANT WATCHMEN

The Bible has plenty to say about the greedy man. Greedy prophets lay wait and lurk privily (Proverbs 1:18-20). The Message Bible translation says they are "racing to a very bad end, hurrying to ruin everything they lay hands on, and robbing a bank while everyone is watching." Greedy prophets trouble their own house (Proverbs 15:27). And Isaiah offers a horrifying look at the greedy watchman. As you read this Scripture, keep in mind that part of the prophetic post is to serve as a watchman.

> "His watchmen are blind: they are all ignorant, they are all dumb dogs, they cannot bark; sleeping, lying down, loving to slumber. Yea, they are greedy dogs which can never have enough, and they are shepherds that cannot understand: they all look to their own way, every one for his gain, from his quarter" (Isaiah 56:10-11).

What good is a blind, ignorant prophet who can't sound the alarm? I believe greed – the lust of the eyes – blinds us to what the Spirit of the Lord is really saying and doing because it's filtered through a desire for profit. Greedy prophets aren't seeing or saying right. Their utterances are muddied by their insatiable desire for their own way and their own gain. They misinterpret – or flat out fabricate – what the Lord is saying because their ears are full of cha-ching sounds that drown out all else.

Ezekiel hits the same greedy spirit, rebuking those who "hast greedily gained of thy neighbors by extortion" (Ezekiel 22:11). Extortion isn't only for gun-toting Mafiosos with pin-stripped suits and Italian accents like we see in gangster movies of old. Extortion means to obtain from a person by force, intimidation, or undue illegal power – or to gain especially by ingenuity or compelling argument.[13] In other words, extortion can be charismatically subtle. Greedy prophets misuse their power – they use undue illegal power – to wring money from your wallet.

EDISON'S MOVIE MONOPOLY

I'm reminded of Thomas Edison and his movie monopoly. Most of you remember Edison as the inventor of the light bulb. That he was, and he was a great inventor indeed. What many don't know is Edison also held patents on motion picture film manufacturing. Unfortunately, it seems greed got the best of him.

Here's the story: Edison hooked up with several other leading motion picture companies to form a film trust called the Motion Picture Patents Company in 1908. The alliance ended the patent wars and litigation that characterized the early days of the film industry. These industry behemoths, though, set out to take dominion by pooling their interests and locking out anybody and everybody who wasn't part of their clique. Greed entered into the picture and the group demanded licensing fees from independent film producers, distributors and exhibitors.

Unwilling to pay tribute, the "unlicensed outlaws" protested the scheme and continued producing films. Greed then inspired Edison and his cohorts to form a strong-arm subsidiary know as the General Film Company for the sole purpose of blocking the independents. The group used coercive tactics that are infamous in the film industry history books. General Film, for instance, confiscated unlicensed equipment and stopped allowing theaters to show its films on the same screens as independent works. Greed led to the Edison movie monopoly. Only William Fox, an early pioneer associated with today's 20th Century Fox, stood against it.

Long story short, as the independents laid the foundation for the modern-day Hollywood scene with a marketable star system and a long-film format, the Motion Picture Patents Company was about to reap a harvest on the seeds of greed and strong-arm tactics it sowed. In 1915, U.S. courts determined Edison's movie monopoly restrained trade and ordered it disbanded. Edison and his cohorts went out of business. The independents, meanwhile, thrived. The moral of the story: Greed always loses in the end.

It seems some prophets and prophetic camps believe they have a monopoly on the word of the Lord. I've spoken to some so-called apostles and prophets one-to-one, ear-to-ear, who have boldly told me things like, "Prophet So-and-So proclaimed this and such and we are not to question it." Others seem to believe that if they pronounce it the rest of the Body of Christ should not only agree without judging the utterance, but should also support it financially – and liberally. Still other prophets expect exorbitant honorariums for their exhortations, tainted as they often are.

Don't get me wrong, I believe in honorariums to visiting ministers and supporting our men and women of God in the local church, but demanding exceedingly exorbitant honorariums, limousines and travel expenses for your whole company seems a bit much in exchange for bringing forth the Word of the Lord. Jesus said we have received freely and we should give freely (Matthew 10:8). Honorariums are often appropriate, but greedy demands are not. Jesus warned against greed:

> "Guard yourselves and keep free from all covetousness (the immoderate desire for wealth, the greedy longing to have more); for a man's life does not consist in and is not derived from possessing overflowing abundance or that which is over and above his needs" (Isaiah 56:10-11 AMP)

Do you take Jesus' warnings seriously? The Prophet is warning us to guard ourselves from greed and keep ourselves free from all covetousness for a good reason – it defiles our hearing, seeing and saying. If you are attaining self-worth or measuring the success of your ministry by the size of your offerings, then you are missing it. John the Baptist didn't haul in six-figure offerings and Jesus said there was not a greater prophet among those born of women (Luke 7:24-28). It's not about the size of the crowd or the size of your church coffers. It's about the size of your God and His will – despite the cost. It's about letting the Holy Spirit have His way free of charge. It's about giving Jesus a platform to speak to His Church prophetically without a price tag.

ELISHA'S UNSELFISHNESS

Selflessness will take you a long way with God. Selfishness will take you nowhere in a hurry. Greed errs to the latter. Consider Elisha, who sacrificed much to pour water over the hands of Elijah (2 Kings 3:11). John the Baptist may have been the greatest prophet, but Elisha was pretty powerful himself. Elisha received a double portion of the Prophet Elijah's anointing and did twice as many miracles as his prophetic mentor. In Elisha you could not find one fiber of greed. It appears that Elisha enjoyed a wealthy upbringing, evidenced by the fact that the family had 12 teams of oxen. He left it all to serve the Lord (1 Kings 19:19-21). In fact, he burned his bridges, so to speak, by burning the oxen. He started his ministry giving. Instead of selling the oxen, he burned them and fed the people.

Unfortunately, Elisha's own protégé, Gehazi, didn't carry that same unselfish spirit. Despite the fact that Gehazi had just witnessed God use Elisha as an instrument to raise the Shunammite woman's son from the dead, and despite the fact that he had stood by as God used Elisha in Naaman's cleansing from leprosy, and despite the fact that Elisha had not accepted any man's reward for either act, Gehazi's greed overtook him.

Allow me to set the scene. Naaman humbled himself and dipped in the Jordan River seven times according to Elisha's word. His flesh became brand new again, like a child's. He was cleansed. Naaman acknowledged God and offered to bless Elisha. But the unselfish prophet said, "As the Lord liveth, before whom I stand, I will receive none" (2 Kings 5:16). Naaman urged him a second time to accept compensation for his miracle-working instructions. But Elisha a second time refused. Naaman then vowed to serve the Lord wholeheartedly, which surely delighted Elisha more than any gold, silver or raiment.

GEHAZI'S GREEDY DISPOSITION

But Naaman's vow to serve the Lord didn't satisfy Gehazi's greedy heart. Let's look at the plain English translation of what happened next, straight from the Message Bible.

"But [Naaman] hadn't gone far when Gehazi, servant to Elisha the Holy Man, said to himself, 'My master has let this Aramean Naaman slip through his fingers without so much as a thank-you. By the living God, I'm going after him to get something or other from him!" And Gehazi took off after Naaman.

"Naaman saw him running after him and jumped down from his chariot to greet him, "Is something wrong? Nothing's wrong, but something's come up. My master sent me to tell you: 'Two young men just showed up from the hill country of Ephraim, brothers from the guild of the prophets. Supply their needs with a gift of 75 pounds of silver and a couple of sets of clothes.' Naaman said, 'Of course, how about a 150 pounds?' Naaman insisted. He tied up the money in two sacks and gave him the two sets of clothes; he even gave him two servants to carry the gifts back with him. "When they got to the fort on the hill, Gehazi took the gifts from the servants, stored them inside, then sent the servants back" (2 Kings 5:20-24).

This was Gehazi's great test and he failed miserably. He not only let greed get the best of him, he lied about it. When he returned to the camp, Elisha asked him straight up: "Where have you been, Gehazi?" The brazen young man replied, "Your servant didn't go anywhere." Elisha told him that he was with Gehazi in spirit when Naaman stepped down from his chariot. In other words, the Lord revealed to Elisha that Gehazi had lined his pockets with gifts. His punishment? Gehazi and his family were stricken with leprosy. Gehazi walked away, his skin flaky and white like snow.

God will test our hearts and minds (Psalm 7:9). God discerns the thoughts and intents of the heart (Hebrews 4:12). God knows everything. If we misuse our prophetic authority, there will be grave consequences – sooner or later. One sin seems to lead to another sin, then to another and another. While Elisha showed kindness to a Syrian, an enemy of Israel, he was forced to pronounce a curse on a fellow Israelite for his greedy, lying disposition. It may have actually been God's mercy because Gehazi was well on the road to false prophethood.

ONE ROOT OF FALSE PROPHECY

When the Apostle Paul outlined the qualifications of a minister of the Gospel to his spiritual son Timothy, he twice mentioned the need to be greed-free.

Specifically, he made it clear that a minister should not be "greedy of filthy lucre" (1 Timothy 3:3, 8). The Amplified Bible says a minister should not be a "lover of money [insatiable for wealth and ready to obtain it by questionable means]" and the Message flat out says we shouldn't be "money-hungry."

You can't be money-hungry and Spirit-hungry at the same time. You can't serve both God and mammon. I know this is Christianity 101, but if the lust of the eyes – greed – wasn't an effective strategy against prophets then the Bible wouldn't repeatedly warn us about it, would it? Greed is dangerous because it opens the door to other sins such as envy, covetousness and merchandising. (We'll discuss merchandising in the next chapter.)

When you envy someone, you resent what they have be it spiritual or temporal. That can thrust you into what I call prophetic envy and prophetic competition. Prophetic envy is when you are jealous of another's prophetic gift, or the material fruits that it produces, and begin to compete with them in true one-upsmanship style. This leads to an "anything you can do I can do better" attitude that escorts error into your midst because the competitor is no longer being lead by the Spirit of God, but by the spirits of envy and religion. Prophets must trust God in and for all things, gifts, callings, and provision. You name it.

Greed can also open the door of the sin of covetousness. The Bible says we should covet prophecy, but it does not say we should covet financial gain or popularity from prophecy. One of the Ten Commandments says, "Thou shalt not covet," does it not? Covetousness is an unusually strong desire for something that belongs to someone else, usually wealth or possessions or power. It's basically a fancier word for bad old-fashioned greed. We know that the love of money is the root of evil. It's also one of the roots lodged deep in the souls of false prophets. The Lord exposed covetousness as one root of a false prophet through the words He sent unto Jeremiah:

> "For every one from the least even unto the greatest is given to covetousness, from the prophet even unto the priest every one dealeth falsely" (Jeremiah 8:10).

Greed is not part of God's nature. God is a giver. Greed is part of the deceitful lusts of the carnal nature. That's why Jude pronounced woe on those false ministers who ran greedily after the error of Balaam for reward and perished in the gainsaying of Khora (Jude 11). What was the error of Balaam? He was a greedy, power hungry merchandiser. God sees it all, though, and we need to see it too because it is a prophetic pothole the size of Texas.

WHO'S WILL: GREED'S OR GOD'S?

Riches are deceitful in that mammon attempts to dictate your every move. Mammon will tell you whether you can give to an evangelistic endeavor. What do you think mammon's answer would be? Mammon will tell you if you can sow into the life of a visiting minister. What do you think mammon's answer would be?

God created mammon to meet our needs, to give to others in need, and to finance the Gospel of the Kingdom. Unfortunately, the devil uses it as a tool to deceive the saints. Greed compounds this deception, for it's one thing to be deceived by a bank account that commands overtime wages to pay the bills. It's another altogether to be deceived by a swelling bank account that has an insatiable desire for more.

Greed can take the place of God in your life. In other words, you will begin to follow the screaming voice of greed rather than the still small voice of God.

Of course, greed enters in subtly, just like any other sin. It may begin with a felt need to keep up with the Joneses, or in this case, keeping up with Prophet Jones who dons $2,000 suits, wears a Rolex and drives a Benz. There's nothing wrong with fancy suits and cars. It's coveting them that is an issue.

THE GREED TEST

Lot's greedy disposition led him away from godly relationships into the heart of the world's sin. He chose all the plain of Jordan (Genesis 13:10-11). The Rich Young Ruler was too greedy to follow the Lord (Mark 10:17-30). Judas Iscariot was greedy enough to crucify Him. What about you? Do you have traces of greed in your heart? And how could you tell if you did? There are a few telltale signs of greed.

1. Do you tithe? If you don't, that may not automatically mean you are greedy. It may be that you aren't trusting God. But let me say this: If you don't trust God with the money in your pocket, then how can He trust you with the money in His? God is the provider. It all belongs to Him anyway. We are just stewards.

If you aren't tithing, it could indeed be a sign that greed has overtaken you. If so, God can't trust you with money.

2. Are you money-minded? Always concerned about how to get more? If so, it could be possible that you are flowing in greed. It depends, of course, on your motive. If you are looking to accumulate more money for orphans in Nicaragua or to otherwise further God's will, then most likely that's not greed. Even still, check your heart because even good motives can turn sour faster than milk on a hot tin roof.

3. Do you compare your possessions with the Joneses? In other words, do you look at your clothes, car, home and other possessions and wish you had what Prophetess Prosperous has? Does it make you angry that Prophet Jones has more than you and isn't as godly as you (in your self-righteous opinion)? Do you try to book more meetings or write more books to accumulate more money so you can get more than what they have? We know that this is not God's way. It's greed's way. What's

more, the Bible says it's not wise to compare.

4.   Do you often struggle between doing God's work, which may not always yield immediate money, and doing the world's work, which may bring in a boatload of cash? There are tests that come your way and God is watching to see what you will choose. If you are greedy, you will always choose the path that leads to those deceitful riches, having been deceived by them.

FREEDOM FROM GREED

If you see greed in your heart, repent. Change your thinking. The Bible offers a prescription for deliverance from greed. It also happens to be preventative medicine that will keep you free from greed in the first place. So whether you have fallen into this snare or just want to clear the path so that you do not, allow the Word of God to speak to your heart:

"But seek ye first the kingdom of God, and his righteousness; and all these things shall be added unto you" (Matthew 6:33).

We need to move in the opposite spirit to break greed's back. When you hear that voice or feel an inclination in your soul to do things greed's way, purposely do just the opposite. If that voice says, "Don't give," then give double. If that voice says, "You don't have time to do God's work today," then spend twice as much time doing God's work this week. Whatever voice that you hear that is not God's voice, make it a general rule to do the very opposite. That is spiritual warfare, friends, and therein lies victory.

Greed brings with it anxiety, dissatisfaction, and oftentimes sorrow. Let me put it another way. The wages of greed is death. In the next chapter, we'll take a closer look at the merchandising spirit that grows from greed.

PROPHETIC KEYS

♦   Greed is when you want more than you need because you are just plain selfish. Greed wants to keep up with the Joneses. Greed may also be a manifestation of distrust in God as your provider.

♦   I believe greed – the lust of the eyes – blinds us to what the Spirit of the Lord is really saying and doing because it's filtered through a desire for profit. Greedy prophets aren't seeing or saying right. Their utterances are muddied by their insatiable desire for their own way and their own gain.

◆ Do you take Jesus' warnings seriously? The Prophet is warning us to guard ourselves from greed and keep ourselves free from all covetousness for a good reason – it defiles our hearing, seeing and saying. If you are attaining your self-worth or measuring the success of your ministry by the size of your offerings, then you are missing it.

◆ God will test our hearts and minds (Psalm 7:9). God discerns the thoughts and intents of the heart (Hebrews 4:12). God knows everything. If we misuse our prophetic authority, there will be grave consequences – sooner or later. One sin seems to lead to another sin, then to another and another.

◆ You can't be money-hungry and Spirit-hungry at the same time. You can't serve both God and mammon. I know this is Christianity

101, but if the lust of the eyes – greed – wasn't an effective strategy against prophets then the Bible wouldn't repeatedly warn us about it, would it?

♦ We need to move in the opposite spirit to break greed's back. When you hear that voice or feel an inclination in your soul to do things greed's way, purposely do just the opposite. If that voice says, "Don't give," then give double.

Chapter 9

THE MERCHANDISING PROPHET

Cure the sick, raise the dead, cleanse the lepers, drive out demons. Freely (without pay) you have received, freely (without charge) give (Matthew 10:8 AMP).

They called him the Rattle Snake King, but his real name was Clark Stanley. He was famous for propagating snake oil cures for anything that ails you, from sciatica to soar throat and scores more. Indeed, he built a snake oil empire, complete with mega manufacturing plants, to bottle his liniment. He truly believed snake oil could cure folk. He was deceiving because he was deceived. It's important to note that the snake oil salesmen that came after Stanley weren't deceived. While Stanley truly believed in the power of the snake oil to heal, the salesmen that rose up to get in on the snake oil game were just trying to earn a quick buck by selling "cures" that they knew were nothing more than colored or scented water.

All sorts of merchandising quacks have traveled the United States with "snake oil" cures over the centuries. Today, some merchandising prophets, with their miracle water, prophetic soap and prosperity oil, are catching naïve Christians hook, line and sinker. Other Gospel gainsayers are profiting with urgent announcements that God will heal the first five people who run up to the altar with $1,000 bill in hand. Television and mail order prophets also abound advertising operator-manned, toll-free numbers to take your prayer requests. These man-made prophetic words are conjured up in a kettle fired by greed with a goal to get money out of your pocket.

> "And through covetousness shall they with feigned words make merchandise of you: whose judgment now of a long time lingereth not, and their damnation slumbereth not" (2 Peter 2:4).

The Message Bible puts it this way:

"They give the way of truth a bad name. They're only out for themselves. They'll say anything, anything, that sounds good to exploit you. They won't, of course, get by with it. They'll come to a bad end, for God has never just stood by and let that kind of thing go on" (2 Peter 2:4 MSG)

These merchandisers will say anything. Sometimes their claims aren't even based on common sense. I was watching Christian television late one night, for instance, and the preacher was extolling his healing powers. He was telling the viewing audience how this famous preacher had prophesied over him and some other famous preacher had imparted anointings to him. He claimed to have one of the most unusual and powerful anointings any man had ever carried. He offered, for free mind you, to send his viewers a piece of the prayer shawl he wore as he consecrated himself to the Lord, along with some holy oil. (What the bewitching broadcaster didn't tell viewers was that they'd be added to a mailing list to be merchandised from that day until Jesus came back.) The merchandisers claimed hundreds had already called for their 2-inch-by-2-inch piece of consecrated prayer shawl. But I had to wonder how big this shawl really was. If hundreds of people really called in, there would not have been anything left to give out. Anyone who thought about it logically would have caught on.

If that wasn't ridiculous enough, shortly thereafter, I received what appeared to be junk mail from another organization that instructed me to stare directly into the eyes of a paper-made "rug" that depicted the face of Jesus. God only knows why they wanted recipients to stare into the eyes of this rendition of His dear Son. It then instructed the reader to send an offering, along with the rug, so they could redistribute it to someone else. Then and only then, the letter instructed, was the reader granted permission to open up a sealed "prophetic word just for you." The letter warned the reader not to break the seal on the envelope containing the prophetic word if they had no intention of cooperating with the rest of the instructions, i.e. to send money. It didn't flat out say it, but the insinuation was that something unpleasant would result in disobeying this process. It was nothing more than a glorified, merchant-inspired faux-Christian chain letter.

I won't even get into the Internet sites that offer a prophetic word in exchange for $50. Of course, they don't put it that way. It's a suggested offering much like what you encounter at the entrance of a museum. The difference is, you can go into the museum whether you pay or not. If you don't send your $50 via check, debit card or PayPal, though, you won't get your prophetic word. Who wants it anyway? These types of activities reduce the prophetic ministry to phone psychics that tap their crystal ball and Tarot cards for 99 cents a minute. The only difference is phone psychics with accents often offer less expensive spiritual counsel. You've probably heard it said that money can't buy happiness. Well, I'm here to tell you that it can't buy a prophetic word, either. Pastors, don't invite merchandisers to preach in your church!

Now, let me be sure you understand. There is a significant difference between merchandisers and men and women of God who sell valuable training resources to support their ministries and the Kingdom of God. For many prophets, offering books, tapes and other Spirit-filled training resources is the best way for them to finance their ministries. And thank God for these stable, balanced resources that equip believers for the work of the ministry. There is absolutely nothing wrong with selling merchandise to support one's ministry because honorariums don't always cover travel expenses much less offer 'more than enough' to support the prophet's family. I know one prophet who gives 50 percent of his income to the Kingdom. Much of that money goes to financing missions around the world. Can you see the difference? Selling merchandise and being a merchandiser, then, are two different lanes on the prophetic highway. Let's stay on the righteous side of the road.

TAPPING INTO DIVINATION

Man-made hype presented as the anointing surely grieves the Holy Spirit. But perhaps the most dangerous merchandisers are those who use their gift to tap into divination. These prophets announce what the believer wants to hear in order to sow a false seed of faith and reap an improper financial reward, inappropriately earned position or wrongly received recognition. No matter the merchandiser's brand of deceit, it is a practice that stinks in the nostrils of God.

> "Then the Lord said, 'These prophets are telling lies in my name. I did not send them or tell them to speak. I did not give them any messages. They prophesy of visions and revelations they have never seen or heard. They speak foolishness made up in their own lying hearts. Therefore, says the Lord, I will punish these lying prophets, for they

have spoken in my name even though I never sent them. They say that no war or famine will come, but they themselves will die by war and famine!'" (Jeremiah 14:14-15)

Of course, most false prophets don't start their ministries as false prophets, rather they are tempted and enticed by the idolatry in their hearts. Avoiding Satan's snare begins with the fear of the Lord and the promised wisdom that follows. After all, the merchandise of wisdom is better than the merchandise of silver, and the gain thereof than fine gold. Not only is it better, it's not going to usher you into sin. Wisdom is more precious than rubies and all the things that you can desire are not to be compared to her (Proverbs 3:14-15).

BALAAM: A MULISH MERCHANDISER

The wisdom in God's Word plainly illustrates that with every temptation there is also a way of escape. By comparing the responses of Balaam with Daniel and of Jezebel's diviners with Elijah, we get a clear view of the trap, the way escape – and the ultimate fate of merchandising prophets.

Balaam is best remembered for his talking donkey. He was a true prophet of God who went the way of divination for the promise of financial gain when King Balak offered him rewards to curse Israel. But Balaam did not fall into sin upon the first temptation. In fact, he refused the king's initial offer. His royal majesty then upped the ante, promising the prophet promotion, honor and power if he would curse the Israelites.

In his book, "Prophetic Operations," Jonas Clark offers some valuable insight into the demonic assignment to pull God's prophets into divination:[14]

"For I will promote thee. Can you see the p-u-l-l of these assignments against the prophet of God? Can you see the demonic enticements released against this prophet? Power, money, honor, prestige, enticements with smooth flattering sayings from the King's most honorable representatives. These are all high level demonic assignments designed to pull on any common ground the devil can find in the heart of God's prophet."

Indeed, besides greed, power, honor and prestige are prophetic pitfalls that can lead the prophet into divination. The Bible says that Balaam once again refused, saying,

> "If Balak would give me his house full of silver and gold, I cannot go beyond the word of the Lord my God, to do less or more" (Numbers 22:18).

Despite his bold confession to obey the Lord's will, Balaam secretly desired to attain the rewards pledged by the king. And so the testing begins. Balaam would follow his rebellious heart 320 miles on a donkey's back to curse Israel and claim his coveted merchandise. But to his surprise, the Lord would not allow him to pronounce the curse when he arrived in Moab. Disappointed and still hoping to collect the king's bribe, Balaam shared a strategy to trip up the Israelites through sexual sin that led to the downfall of his brethren.

Balaam had a clear way of escape: telling the king's messengers upon their first visit that the Lord forbid him to curse Israel. That would have probably closed the door to future offers and put an end to the temptation that would lead to his destruction. The end of Balaam came at the sword of his own people through the command of Moses, the Israelites he tried to curse through divination.

DANIEL'S DEDICATION

Daniel, on the other hand, refused to give in to the temptation presented in King Belshazzar's dilemma. Belshazzar and his guests were drinking from gold and silver cups that his father had stolen from God's temple. The group was giving praises to idols when the fingers of a human hand appeared and wrote on the palace wall. Belshazzar was frightened and summoned enchanters, fortunetellers and diviners to come, promising riches and power to anyone who could interpret it. When none could, the king called Daniel and made him the same offer (Daniel 5).

Daniel was faced with three choices at this critical turning point in his ministry. He could accept the king's offer to interpret the message, thereby merchandising his gifting. He could exercise the gift he had freely received from Jehovah to freely interpret the message, all the while knowing that such a harsh word from the Lord could land him in the lion's den. Or he could stand on his credible reputation as God's prophet to falsely interpret the warning message as a blessing message and in all likelihood collect the loot anyway.

Unlike Balaam, Daniel unlocked the hard truth in the writing on the wall. He told the king that his days were numbered and that his kingdom would be divided up and handed over to enemies. Daniel refused to compromise, no matter the consequences, and God used the king to promote him. As one of his last acts as king, Belshazzar robed Daniel in purple, draped the great gold chain around his neck and positioned him as third-in-charge of the kingdom.

ELIJAH VS.
850 FALSE PROPHETS

King Ahab and his wife Jezebel took the tradition of kings calling on prophets to unlock the mysteries of God a step further – and a few steps too far. Jezebel had false prophets on her payroll. The wicked queen regularly fed 450 prophets of Baal and 400 prophets of Asherah. Bible scholars estimate that feeding those false prophets cost her about $12,750 a week or $663,000 a year. That's a hefty price tag for a good prophetic word.

So while Jezebel's prophets had full bellies in a time of famine, the queen cut off the prophets of the Lord for fear of the truth (1 Kings 18:4). Obadiah, a type of religious spirit, hid 100 of God's prophets in caves and fed them bread and water. While this may appear like a good work on the surface, Obadiah was only facilitating Jezebel's plan to cut off the uncompromising prophetic word.

While Jezebel's prophets looked well-fed and God's true prophets looked like sheep being led to the slaughter, the story changes in a hurry when Elijah confronts the 850 merchandisers at Mount Carmel in what goes down in Biblical history as the ultimate showdown between the true and the false. Elijah threw down the prophetic gauntlet and challenged the false camp to bring fire down from heaven by calling upon their god. The merchandising diviners cried to Baal from dawn to dusk with no answer.

When the false camp had finally exhausted itself, Elijah built an altar holding a sacrifice to Jehovah, drenched it with four barrels of water, said a simple prayer, and watched as the fire of God fell from heaven and consumed the sacrifice, the wood, the stones, the dust and even the water in the trench. Then Elijah's false counterparts were slain one by one. So the ultimate fate of the false prophets came at the hand of the true prophet, who was later taken to heaven in a chariot of fire.

MODERN-DAY TEMPTATIONS

Like Old Testament prophets, modern-day prophets are also being tempted to merchandise the anointing for fame, fortune or friends in high places. Being plugged into a strong local apostolic church is a safety net because true apostles boldly confront false moves of the Spirit and give merchandisers a way of escape by leading them into deep repentance.

Recall Simon the sorcerer, who was highly esteemed among the Samarians because he bewitched them. The apostles Peter and John met up with Simon after praying for the baptism of the Holy Ghost for the new believers there. When Simon saw that the people were filled with the Spirit when the apostles laid their hands on them, he offered them money.

"Saying, Give me also this power, that on whomsoever I lay hands, he may receive the Holy Ghost. But Peter said unto him, Thy money perish with thee, because thou hast thought the gift of God may be purchased with money. Thou hast neither part nor lot in this matter: for thy heart is not right in the sight of God" (Acts 8:19-21).

Simon repented and asked the apostles to pray for him. This is the appropriate response for New Testament prophets who fall into the trap of merchandising.

The decision to go the way of Baal and or to go the way of Elijah lies in the prophet's heart. If self-will, anger, or lust occupies the place where obedience, love and truth should live, then the merchandising prophet may succeed in reaping worldly rewards for a season but the retirement fund built on ill-gotten gains leads only to death (Romans 6:23). While there is certainly abundant grace for the true prophet who misses it, the Book of Revelation makes it clear that the false prophets (those who purposely set out to lie and deceive God's people) will be cast into the lake of fire and brimstone and be tormented day and night forever and ever (Revelation 20:10).

PROPHETIC KEYS

+ All sorts of merchandising quacks have traveled the United States with "snake oil" cures over the centuries. Today, some merchandising prophets, with their miracle water, prophetic soap and prosperity oil, are catching naïve Christians hook, line and sinker.

+ Man-made hype surely grieves the Holy Spirit. But perhaps the most dangerous merchandisers are those who use their gift to tap into divination.

♦ Avoiding Satan's snare begins with the fear of the Lord and the promised wisdom that follows. After all, the merchandise of wisdom is better than the merchandise of silver, and the gain thereof than fine gold.

♦ Like Old Testament prophets, modern-day prophets are also being tempted to merchandise the anointing for fame, fortune or friends in high places. Being plugged into a strong local apostolic church is a safety net because true apostles boldly confront false moves of the Spirit and give merchandisers a way of escape by leading them into deep repentance.

♦ The decision to go the way of Baal and or to go the way of Elijah lies in the prophet's heart. If self-will, anger, or lust occupies the place where obedience, love and truth should live, then the merchandising prophet may succeed in reaping worldly rewards for a season but the retirement fund built on ill-gotten gains leads only to death (Romans 6:23).

Chapter 10

THE DECEITFUL PROPHET

The heart is hopelessly dark and deceitful, a puzzle that no one can figure out. But I, God, search the heart and examine the mind. I get to the heart of the human. I get to the root of things. I treat them as they really are, not as they pretend to be (1 Samuel 15:23 MSG).

It's the little foxes that spoil the vine (Song of Solomon 2:15). If you give the devil a millimeter, he'll take a mile. There is no such thing as a white lie. They all spring from the kingdom of darkness. Compromise may be an admirable word in Corporate

America but it can be a curse to the prophetic ministry. Oh, what a tangled web we weave when first we practice to deceive.

Have I given you enough clichés to adequately paint the picture?

I'm talking about integrity, honesty...incorruptibility. Integrity is mortar in the foundation of every powerful prophet. Deceit is mixed in the mortar of every false one. You know, I don't believe false prophets start off as false prophets. I believe they compromise their integrity at some point along the supernatural highway. Instead of keeping their eyes on the prize and refusing to look to the right (where the fame is) or to the left (where the fortunes are) they take a sudden, sharp turn – or even make a 180-degree spin – and head in the opposite direction of God's Spirit. (That's what stubborn Prophet Jonah did and we all know where that landed him.)

In our study of character flaws that leave devil-sized cracks, it's important to examine the derivation of deceit. It's also important to discuss how to avoid it. Rather than perishing in a false prophetic flow, God can exalt us to serve as credible voices that speak into nations, governments and the kingdoms. He can use us to bring lasting reformation – if we have clean hearts.

WHICH SEED WILL YOU SOW?

Faith is often compared to a grain of mustard seed. Jesus told His disciples if they had just a teeny tiny bit of faith, they could command a mountain to be moved – and it would move. Jesus later likens the Kingdom of God to a mustard seed, which, when it is sown in the earth is less than all the seeds that are in the earth. But when it is sown, it grows up and becomes greater than all the herbs and shoots out huge branches (Mark 4:31-32). That's how it works in the Kingdom of Light.

I submit to you that a white lie, a microscopic compromise, a seemingly insignificant exaggeration could also be likened to a grain of mustard seed. It may seem like a relatively innocent act – or at least not a monumental sin – but it can cause you to wind up in the depths of the valley when you should be successfully commanding mountains to move. When the seeds of lies, compromise and exaggerations are sown, it may seem like a small thing. But if you don't repent of it, it can lead you down the detour of deceit and into the realm of false prophecy.

WHAT EXACTLY IS A LIE?

Deceit is the deliberate act or practice of deceiving, misleading, tricking, or defrauding.[15] Lying is making an untrue statement with the intent to deceive or to create a false or misleading impression.[16] Many deceitful practices entail lying – and every single one of them is motivated by hell's prince.

The Bible clearly states that Satan is the father of all lies (John 8:44). All lies means all lies, white, black or whatever shade you want to color them. When you make an untrue statement with intent to deceive, you are lying. That means when you told the pastor the traffic was so bad last Sunday morning that it caused you to be late for corporate prayer, but in reality you just didn't feel like getting up on time, you lied.

Let's go a little further, keeping in mind Jesus is looking at the heart and not merely the letter of the law. It was Jesus who compared hateful thoughts to murder and lustful thoughts to adultery. So when you create a false or misleading impression you are also lying. It's a matter of the heart. That means even if the traffic was bad on the way to church you are still setting out to deceive because the truth is that if you had gotten up on time then you wouldn't have got stuck in traffic to begin with.

Can I take you just one step further, now? Just because you don't open your mouth and commit a lie doesn't let you off the hook, either. Omitting the truth can also be a lie if your motive is to deceive. I'm telling you the truth in Christ. Do you think Jesus would have told a white lie? He is the Truth.

A lying tongue and a false witness that speaks lies are two of the seven abominations Solomon lists by the inspiration of the Holy Spirit in the sixth chapter of Proverbs. Both abominations are coated with deceit. The Apostle Paul warns his spiritual son Timothy that those who live a godly life will be persecuted, but "wicked men and imposters will go on from bad to worse, deceiving and leading astray others and being deceived and led astray themselves" (2 Timothy 3:13 AMP). Sounds akin to a false prophet to me.

Don't be deceived. God is not mocked. Whatever a man sows that he will also reap. At the end of the day, if you set out to deceive you set yourself up for a great deception: "A wicked doer giveth heed to false lips; and a liar giveth ear to a naughty tongue" (Proverbs 17:4). Deceitfulness opens the door to the devil and muddies your prophetic flow.

FALSE OR INACCURATE?

Many bona fide prophets have been accused of prophesying falsely because their utterance did not come to pass. Sure, a prophet's track record is important and one who continually misses the mark either isn't a prophet at all or needs some help from more mature prophetic ministers to get to the root of the problem. But "missing it" in and of itself does not make someone a false prophet. If prophets were 100 percent accurate 100 percent of the time, people would follow prophets instead of following Jesus. This is why all prophecy needs to be judged.

A false prophet is one who deliberately practices deception. That means they set out to deceive on a regular basis. Since the wicked doer gives heed to false lips and a liar gives ear to a naughty tongue, you can see the cycle of deception that occurs. The prophet may have told a white lie or made a small compromise and failed to repent of the wicked work. He feels bad about it, but doesn't truly change his thinking. He does it over and over again. He doesn't see the potential pothole on his prophetic highway.

Soon, he begins to exaggerate about some spiritual experience he had to make a point. Later, the Holy

Spirit brings it to his attention, but he shirks it off, failing to repent (to change his thinking). Eventually, the prophet no longer feels bad about the lies he is speaking and teaching and the wickedness finds a place in his prophetic flow. The Apostle Paul warned Timothy about these types of ministers:

> "Now the Spirit expressly declares that in later times some will fall away from the faith, giving heed to deceiving spirits and the teachings of demons; through the hypocrisy of men who teach falsely and have their own consciences seared as with a hot iron..." (1 Timothy 4:1-2 WEYMOUTH)

ROOTING OUT THE MOTIVE

Every Christian knows lying is wrong, so why does it happen? Lying is part of the carnal nature. We know that just because we are born again doesn't mean our souls – our mind, will and emotions – are born again. Our minds are not automatically renewed at the spiritual rebirth. That means our old soulish ways will remain intact until the engrafted Word saves our souls.

In other words, if we had a tendency to lie and deceive before we were saved – and we all did to some degree, even sweet and innocent children have been known to lie – then we will have that same temptation as born again believers until we renew our minds.

But what does that temptation tap into? In other words, what motivates people to lie? There is no one single motivator and perhaps that's what makes it so difficult to lay the axe to the root of deception. For example, one person might lie because they don't want to hurt someone's feelings. (That's a people-pleasing spirit.) Another person may lie because they fear judgment or punishment. (That's the fear of man.) Yet another person might lie for personal gain. (That's the lust of the eyes.) Another person may lie to avoid rejection. In any case, they aren't trusting God. They are depending on themselves to get through whatever uncomfortable situation they find themselves in, or, by contrast, to take advantage of whatever potentially profitable situation they find themselves in. They lie because they decide not to do things God's way.

If there is a common thread of temptation it's self. Self is the root of so many of our problems. This is illustrated in the Bible. Rahab the harlot lied for self-preservation (Joshua 2:2-7). Jacob and his mother lied to selfishly secure a blessing from God the younger son didn't have a birthright to (Genesis 27). Abraham also lied for self-preservation (Genesis 12:10-13). Samson lied to Delilah about the source of his strength (Judges 16). David lied to the priest while fleeing from Saul (1 Samuel 21:1-2). Peter lied about knowing Jesus (Mark 14).

Some of those lies had extremely negative consequences. David's lie, for example, resulted in the death of an entire family of priests (1 Samuel 22). Jacob's lie caused a long-term rift between he and his brother, Esau. Jacob was exiled from his homeland for more than two decades. Peter's lie caused him great personal turmoil.

WHY DO PEOPLE LIE?

So, again I ask, why do people lie anyway? Well, we see that the root, in one way or another, is self. But let's take a closer look at attitudes about lying as illustrated in an AP-Ipsos poll. The results of this poll of 1,000 adults are telling. About four in 10 believe lying is justified sometime. Fifty-two percent, meanwhile, said it is never justified any of the time. Specifically, 65 percent of those surveyed said it was sometimes alright to lie to avoid hurting someone's feelings. Forty-four percent said it's alright to exaggerate the facts to make a story more interesting while 33 percent think it's OK to lie about being sick in order to play hooky from work. Ten percent believe it's OK to lie to their spouse about an affair.

Just how frequently do people lie? Is it just a once in a while occurrence, or are we lied to each and every day of our lives by someone? Twenty percent of those surveyed had lied during the previous week. (It could be possible that some of the remaining 80 percent who claimed to be truthful were indeed lying.) Thirty-nine percent said they never feel they have to lie or cheat, even just a little. That corresponds closely to the 38 percent of those surveyed who described themselves as born again or evangelical Christians. Isn't that interesting? What's more interesting is this: Nearly one in 10 who said they never have to lie reported in the following question that they might have told a lie in the past week. In other words, they can't even tell the truth in the poll.

Most people lie in everyday conversation when they are trying to appear likable and competent, according to a study conducted by University of Massachusetts psychologist Robert S. Feldman. "People tell a considerable number of lies in everyday conversation. It was a very surprising result," he says. "We didn't expect lying to be such a common part of daily life."

The study also found that lies told by men and women differ in content, though not in quantity. Feldman says the results showed men do not lie more than women or vice versa, but that men and women lie in different ways. "Women were more likely to lie to make the person they were talking to feel good, while men lied most often to make themselves look better," Feldman says.

The lies students told varied considerably, according to Feldman. Some were relatively minor, such as agreeing with the person with whom they were speaking that they liked someone when they really did not. Others were more extreme, such as falsely claiming to be the star of a rock band. "It's so easy to lie," Feldman concludes. "We teach our children that honesty is the best policy, but we also tell them it's polite to pretend they like a birthday gift they've been given. Kids get a very mixed message regarding the practical aspects of lying, and it has an impact on how they behave as adults."

TRUTH OR CONSEQUENCES

What I've noticed is that lies beget lies. In other words, the liar has to tell new lies to cover up for the old lies. If he gets away with it, it encourages him to lie more, premeditating stories to help him reach his goal or to cover up some unseemly mistake. But God is not a man that He should lie (Numbers 23:19). And when we lie – even if no one else ever finds out – we breach God's trust in us.

How can God trust His prophets and intercessors with His secrets if we show ourselves untrustworthy in little things? He who is faithful over little things will have charge over many things (Matthew 25:21). Or, you could put it this way: To whom much is given much is required (Luke 12:48). If you want to walk in high levels of prophetic anointing – if you want that double-portion – then you have to pay the price: faithfulness and honesty.

To bring balance, yes, there is a difference between lying to spare someone's feelings after they got a horrendous haircut and prophesying lies. Prophesying lies causes damage to the prophet and those around him. The consequences, then, are doubly troublesome. Remember the prophet who went to Bethel to prophesy against it (1 Kings 13)? Jeroboam was angry with the prophet and tried to capture him, to no avail. Having successfully accomplished his mission, the young prophet was returning home to Judah when, unfortunately, he ran into an old prophet who prophesied lies:

> "An angel spake unto me by the word of the Lord, saying, Bring him back with thee into thine house, that he may eat bread and drink water. But he lied unto him" (Revelation 21:8).

The Lord specifically told the young prophet not to make any stops on his way back home, but this old prophet spoke lies that caused him to second-guess his prophetic instruction. The young prophet went with his elder counterpart and ate bread and drank water, not knowing it would be his last supper. Then, the Spirit of the Lord came upon the old prophet to predict the young one's doom. Just as the old prophet uttered, a lion ate him when he left.

The moral of the story is that we must follow God's Spirit. This elder prophet wasn't the younger prophet's spiritual covering. The young prophet wasn't accountable to the old prophet. But many of our young prophets today are in danger of being deceived by following the advice of someone who appears to be more mature in the prophetic; who appears to have more experience and wisdom; who appears to be able to make provision for a weary prophetic soldier.

There is a balancing act here. We must respect our elders, but we must not turn off our spiritual discerner, either. Yes, we must submit to our spiritual leaders, but what we do must not violate the Word of God in any instance. Again, this young prophet wasn't accountable to this elder. He met him on his way home from ministering in Bethel. He was probably in a tired, weak and hungry physical condition. He had needs and this older prophet was able to meet those needs, so he gave him an ear and it ended up costing his life.

THE FATE OF DECEIVERS

The Bible has plenty to say about deceitful prophets and we would do well to examine their fate. In the Gospel of Matthew, Jesus warned that many false prophets would arise and deceive many (Matthew 24:11). But He wasn't the first one to sound the alarm to warn people about the deluge of phony five-fold gifts. The Lord warned through Jeremiah that prophets were prophesying lies in His name and said those same prophets would perish by sword and famine because they lied about God's coming judgment (Jeremiah 12:14-16).

Oh, that was the Old Testament, you say? Well, what then will we do with this Scripture from the Book of Revelation that lumps liars with murderers, sorcerers and other especially wicked sinners?

> "But the fearful, and unbelieving, and the abominable, and murderers, and whoremongers, and sorcerers, and idolaters, and all liars, shall have their part in the lake which burneth with fire and brimstone: which is the second death" (Revelation 21:8)

You've probably heard the childhood accusing rhyme "Liar, liar, pants on fire." Now you understand its origin. Make no mistake, the Holy Spirit is the ultimate lie detector. He doesn't rely on an injection of truth serum or some newfangled technology to measure your heart rate under interrogation. He sees the inward parts and desires truth (Psalm 51:6). Lying prophets may fool some of the people some of the time, but they won't fool God any of the time. Instead, they will make themselves as fools.

AVOIDING DECEPTION

Look, God holds teachers (and prophets who teach the Word) to a higher standard than others. That's why James, the apostle of practical faith, warned, "Not many of you should presume to be teachers, my brothers, because you know that we who teach will be judged more strictly" (James 3:1 NIV). Yet, we know that prophets are called to equip (teach) the saints. If we are deceiving and being deceived, we could wind up in the hot seat for eternity. At the very least, it will hinder our prophetic flow.

So how do you avoid this fiery fate? How do you guard yourself from being deceived? By walking in integrity. God's Word is full of integrity from cover to cover. If you compromise on the Word of God, you are setting yourself up for deception. Again, God doesn't expect us to be perfect, but He does expect us to walk in the light we have. Even little children understand that it's wrong to lie.

In his second letter to the church at Corinth, the Apostle Paul said he and his co-laborers in Christ had,

> "renounced the hidden things of dishonesty,
> not walking in craftiness, nor handling the
> word of God deceitfully; but by manifestation

of the truth commending ourselves to every man's conscience in the sight of God" (2 Corinthians 4:2).

Whether you have told what you thought was a simple white lie, exaggerated a spiritual experience, or even handled the Word of God deceitfully, you can renounce the hidden things of dishonesty right now. If you confess your sin, He is faithful and just to forgive you and cleanse you from all unrighteousness. Thank God for His mercy and grace and vow, as Job did, not to compromise your integrity for any price (Job 27:5).

PROPHETIC KEYS

+ Integrity is mortar in the foundation of every powerful prophet. Deceit is mixed in the mortar of every false one.

+ When the seeds of lies, compromise and exaggerations are sown, it may seem like a small thing. But if you don't repent of it, it can lead you down the detour of deceit and into the realm of false prophecy.

+ Many bona fide prophets have been accused of prophesying falsely because their utterance did not come to pass. Sure, a prophet's track record is important and one who continually misses the mark either isn't a prophet at all or needs some help from more mature prophetic ministers to get to the root of the problem. But "missing it" in and of itself does not make someone a false prophet.

+ How can God trust His prophets and intercessors with His secrets if we show ourselves untrustworthy in little things? He who is faithful over little things will have charge over many things (Matthew 25:21). Or, you could put it this way: To whom much is given much is required (Luke 12:48). If you want to walk in high levels of prophetic anointing – if you want that double-portion – then you have to pay the price, faithfulness and honesty.

+ We must respect our elders, but we must not turn off our spiritual discerner, either. Yes, we must submit to our spiritual leaders, but what we do must not violate the Word of God in any instance.

✦   Whether you have told what you thought was a simple white lie, exaggerated a spiritual experience, or even handled the Word of God deceitfully, you can renounce the hidden things of dishonesty right now. If you confess your sin, He is faithful and just to forgive you and cleanse you from all unrighteousness.

Chapter 11

THE JUDGEMENTAL PROPHET

Brothers, do not slander one another. Anyone who speaks against his brother or judges him speaks against the law and judges it. When you judge the law, you are not keeping it, but sitting in judgment on it. There is only one Lawgiver and Judge, the one who is able to save and destroy. But you—who are you to judge your neighbor? (James 4:11-12)

Robertson warns Pennsylvania town of wrath of God[17] Farrakhan says Katrina was wrath of God[18] Pope Benedict XVI warns drug dealers of wrath of God[19]

Gov.: Twister Damage "Wrath of God"[20]
Taiwan politician says AIDS is the wrath of God[21]
Atlanta pastor calls tsunami wrath of God[22]

These are a few of the many news headlines proclaiming God's judgment from sea to shining sea and from one end of the world to the other. Christian leaders, Muslim leaders, Catholic leaders, and U.S. government officials may not have much in common theologically, other than their views on the wrath of God.

Now let's bring it home to prophetic circles. Prophetic camps are clearly at odds over this issue. Some prophets are preaching judgment and others are preaching prosperity. I'll leave it to your discernment to try the spirits (1 John 4:1). But I will tell you this: folks who are prophesying the wrath of God at every turn are discrediting the prophetic in the eyes of both the world and the Church. It's difficult to find a natural disaster, a broken bridge, a high death toll in the media today that some judgmental prophet doesn't take credit for prophesying.

Acts 3:21 says heaven must receive Jesus until…

"the times of restitution of all things, which God hath spoken by the mouth of all his holy prophets since the world began."

If the holy prophets have been speaking about the restitution of all things since the world began, then shouldn't holy prophets still be speaking about the restitution of all things? Restitution is the act of restoring, not the act of destroying. So why do so many prophets prophesy destruction instead of restoration? Let's look at some of the potential pitfalls that could lead prophets to prophesy judgment even when He wants to restore rather than raze.

WHO IS JESUS TO YOU?

Here's the takeaway from this chapter: You will prophesy according to your revelation of who Jesus is. And you can't prophesy beyond your knowledge of Him. Since the spirit of prophecy is the testimony of Jesus, according to Revelation 19:10, then it seems clear your testimony of Jesus will color the spirit of the prophecy you release.

For example, if you think Jesus is sitting in heaven with a huge mallet ready to whack you in the head if you don't toe the line, then your prophecies will be largely corrective, negative and even judgmental in nature because the words of the Lord get filtered through your perception. The Holy Ghost could give you a word of encouragement but your delivery turns it into a word of correction. This is not the spirit of prophecy, which is to edify, comfort and exhort (1 Corinthians 14:3). This is not the testimony Jesus has for His Church.

Yes, there are true corrections and warnings of the Spirit, but I have found these are not the common operations of New Testament prophets or the main function of the spirit of prophecy. At the roots of these negative, judgmental and critical prophecies are frustration, bitterness, pride and rejection, to name a few. If these roots aren't plucked out and filled in with the love of Christ, then our prophetic flow will be stopped up – or at least swimming with unclean things.

JUDGMENTAL AND NEGATIVE

Before we examine some of the roots, let's just review a few verses and insights from respected prophetic leaders on the subject of prophets who deliver critical and judgmental prophecies. In his book, "The Prophetic Ministry,"[23] Rick Joyner points out that even some of the hardest biblical prophecies of impending judgment were tempered with hope and offers of reconciliation for those who repented. However, he adds, we aren't living in Old Testament times anymore. Let's read an excerpt from his text:

"Many today who are called as prophets tried to take on the perceived nature of their Old Testament counterparts, which has often resulted in a distortion of their own calling and nature. True prophets are not by nature critical, judgmental, or harsh! That which is of the Holy Spirit will have the fruit of the Spirit, which is love, joy, peace, patience, kindness, goodness, faithfulness, gentleness and self-control (see Galatians 5:22-23.)".

And, of course, we know that the Apostle James tells us mercy triumphs over judgment (James 2:13). I believe sometimes the Lord will show a prophet what is wrong in someone's life. If the prophet has a critical spirit he will make an announcement declaring the person's woes and what steps he should take to emerge from them in the midst of the congregation. If the prophet has a spirit of mercy, then he will intercede for the saint and talk to him in private about what the Lord has said, if at all. Prophets have no business traveling to churches and delivering critical prophecies to sheep they are not shepherding. Again, prophets are intercessors and when the Lord shows a prophet that a believer is missing it, he shouldn't be quick to judge. He should be quick to show mercy and pray.

PERSECUTED FOR PROPHESYING GOOD

When I interviewed Dr. Bill Hamon, founder of Christian International Ministries and widely considered one of the fathers of the modern day prophetic movement, for an article in *The Voice* magazine, I specifically asked him what he thought of New Testament prophets who exhibited a critical, judgmental spirit. Here's what he said:

> "When I started prophesying the only people that they thought about as prophets were these hard, narrow-minded mean people you see in old movies that had an old legalistic air about them. Some of the biggest persecution that I have got is people saying all I prophesy is good. They told me I ought to rip people apart and judge them and condemn them. They wanted me to blast them, I said, 'No, no, no. The Bible says edify, comfort and encourage.' Some people

just want to bring out all the negative stuff, saying that the only true prophets are John the Baptist prophets that rebuke the Pharisees.'"

Yes, God is still a God of judgment, but Jesus paid the price and took God's wrath upon Himself on that old wooden cross. That's why Dr. Hamon's words were a breath of fresh air and I believe the breath of the Holy Spirit on the subject. However, it is clear that not everyone agrees. There are many reasons prophets get judgmental, critical and negative. We're going to look at a few of them in this chapter.

FRUSTRATED PROPHETS

Let's start with the easy one: frustration. If maturity is the ability to think, speak and act on your feelings within the bounds of dignity, then the measure of maturity is how spiritual you become during the midst of your frustrations. So said 19th century American poet, soldier, civic leader and businessman Samuel Ullman, and it's a saying worthy of reflection.

I've found there to be plenty of frustration in the prophetic ministry. There's the frustration of being misunderstood. The frustration of not being accepted.

The frustration of being flat out rejected. The frustration that those around you don't have spiritual ears and eyes to understand what the Lord is saying. Indeed, there is lots of frustration.

The very definition of frustration[24] perfectly describes the feelings this spirit brings with it: a deep chronic sense or state of insecurity and dissatisfaction arising from unresolved problems or unfilled needs. That's an accurate summation in itself, but there is also a deeper meaning: to balk or defeat in an endeavor; to induce feelings of discouragement in. If that weren't enough, to frustrate also means to make ineffectual and to bring to nothing. Sounds like the devil's plan to me. The overarching purpose of frustration is to hinder you from fulfilling your prophetic destiny (Ezra 4:4).

THE FRUIT OF FRUSTRATION

Few things hinder the grace of God more than frustration. Frustration is not faith. Since Romans 12:6 tells us we should prophesy according to the proportion of our faith, faith-inspired utterances and frustration just don't seem to mix, do they? Indeed, they don't and the fruit of frustration can muddy our prophetic waters.

In his book, "Developing Your Prophetic Gifting,"[25]Graham Cooke offers some interesting insight into negativity and judgmentalism. He calls attention to the importance of avoiding both. If we find it easy to give hard words, he explains, there's something wrong with our spirits. If we find it easy to give negative words, he adds, we have no understanding of the grace and goodness of God. Cooke writes:

> "Frustration is an enemy to the prophetic ministry. It will always color our thinking, infect the word we have and give us a jaundiced perspective on the life of the church. If we are to represent God's heart and be good servants, we must learn to master our frustration. We need the understanding and grace of God to move our hearts rather than our own irritation and dissatisfaction."

To be sure, God's grace is sufficient. We need to lay our frustrations down at His feet before we sit in His counsel so that our prophetic utterances won't come with the wrong types of burdens. Instead of wasting time and energy being agitated by circumstances, we are supposed to offer up prayer and supplication, with thanksgiving, and make our definite requests known to God. Then

God's peace shall be ours and it will guard our hearts and minds in Christ Jesus (Philippians 4:7). That should allow us to pass Ullman's test of thinking, acting and speaking in the Spirit even in the midst of frustration.

LISTEN TO YOUR HEART

Another reason prophets and prophetic believers deliver judgmental, critical or otherwise negative words that are not in line with God's will is because of bitterness. If we speak out of the abundance of our hearts, then our lips tell all that is stored in our soul. James saw the power in the tongue to reveal the innermost recesses of mind. He noted with the tongue we praise our Lord and Father, and with it we curse men, who are made in God's likeness. So out of the same mouth come praises and cursing. He said this should not be so (James 3:9-10). Remember that blessing essentially means to speak well of while cursing means to speak ill of.

James goes on, "Doth a fountain send forth at the same place sweet water and bitter? Can the fig tree, my brethren, bear olive berries? either a vine, figs? so can no fountain both yield salt water and fresh?" (James 3:11-12) James is saying that one source cannot produce two different types water. A bitter, salty source cannot produce sweet, fresh water any more than a fig tree can produce apples. It's just not going to happen. If you've got bitterness in your soul, it's going to infiltrate your prophetic flow, making it pungent.

"If you have bitter jealousy (envy) and contention (rivalry, selfish ambition) in your hearts, do not pride yourselves on it and thus be in defiance of and false to the Truth" (James 3:14 AMP).

In other words, listen to yourself talk. If you know you are bitter, don't try to deny it. If you know your prophetic flow is salty instead of sweet, then don't let your pride keep you from admitting it and wind up deceived. Don't hear this word and ignore it or you could find yourself on the road to false prophethood. If you refuse to deal with character issues like judgment, pride, criticalness and the like, then the wisdom you receive from the spirit realm may come from somewhere other than the Spirit of God much of the time. The judgment and curses you are pronouncing will defy God's truth, not herald it.

HURRICANES, FIRES, EARTHQUAKES AND FLOODS

Now let's get back to the wrath issue. Amid graphic images of New Orleans submerged in lakes of sewage-filled water and horrifying reports of rising death tolls, separated families and traumatized children, many Christians felt the pain of those Hurricane Katrina devastated. I've heard prophet after prophetess take credit for predicting the storm and even claim that the worst natural disaster in American history was Jehovah's judgment on New Orleans, a manifestation of God's wrath against wickedness, and a "spiritual cleansing."

Quite frankly, I am embarrassed by such prophecies. One "prophet" went as far to say that Hurricane Katrina's far-reaching destruction was certainly "the will of God and an answer to prayer." What prophetic spirit is this? I was not surprised that Islamic extremist terrorists are boasting that God has joined their holy jihad against imperialist America, but how can God's prophets claim He causes tragedies like this?

Have we forgotten the mandate of the prophet to intercede? To stand in the gap? To make up the hedge? If prophets did receive a godly warning about a devastating hurricane as long as seven years ago, how come those prophets did not warn the churches in the territory before the storm swallowed up such cities as New Orleans and scattered the faithful servants of our Lord?

Hurricane Katrina should act as a wake up call to America's true prophets and intercessors. It's time to climb up on the watchtower, sound the alarm, and commission the prayer warriors instead of waiting for disaster to strike, reviewing an archive of ambiguous prophetic words of judgment, and looking for one that appears to fit the bill to determine who has bragging rights.

BARS, BROTHELS AND GOVERNING CHURCHES

If Hurricane Katrina was God's judgment on New Orleans, then how come the bars and brothels were open the next day while churches were destroyed? What about all the governing churches in the tri-state region? Did Jesus seek to wipe them out, too? Did God miss? Does He have bad aim? I think not. God didn't send that hurricane, yet I've spoken with apostles and prophets who have called me a fool for saying so.

They rifle through Old Testament Scriptures where prophets demonstrate judgment after judgment as their evidence.

I'm not going to get into a full-blown debate in this book because it's not the purpose of the book to do so. However, claiming that Hurricane Katrina is God's judgment on New Orleans is not biblical and I do not agree with this viewpoint. Prophecies about hurricanes, wildfires and earthquakes abound, and are often declared as God's judgment on sin or disobedience. Surely, God does reveal devastating events to His prophets so we can pray, but it's the spirit behind such judgmental prophetic announcements that is cause for concern.

Since the spirit of prophecy is the testimony of Jesus, are we to conclude that our Lord's will is to pronounce judgment in a time of grace? Jesus came so we could have abundant life (John 10:10). The Apostle Paul said "bless and curse not" (Romans 12:14). The Word says unbelievers are judged already if they don't believe in the Son of God (John 3:18). Does it make sense to pronounce another curse against them? Did Jesus take the sin of the world and experience the wrath of God on behalf of every creature or not? Did His sacrifice satisfy God's wrath or not?

Let me leave you with a couple more questions to consider: Does telling unbelievers that God destroyed their home, killed their children, and left their lives in utter ruin serve His purposes to draw all men to Him? Or does it cause animosity toward the only One who can save them from their misery and sin and restore peace and righteousness to their lives? I think we all know the answer to those questions. I fully intend to continue standing up against the judgment-and-curse camp that is traveling around our nation and publishing books with false prophetic utterances in them. You can count on that. I believe it's rooted in bitterness and that Jezebel has taken advantage of painful wounds in these precious people who are unfortunately prophesying lies.

WHERE IS YOUR WISDOM COMING FROM?

Bitterness, my friends, must be rooted out. If you have bitter envying and strife in your heart, glory not, and lie not against the truth. The Holy Ghost spoke expressly through James that this wisdom is not from God but is earthly, unspiritual and even devlish. Wherever there is envying and strife, there is also confusion and every evil work (James 3:16). God is not the author of confusion or evil works. So if your prophetic utterances are bringing confusion, they are not coming from the expressly-speaking Holy Ghost (1 Timothy 4:1).

> "But the wisdom from above is first of all pure (undefiled); then it is peace-loving, courteous (considerate, gentle). [It is willing to] yield to reason, full of compassion and good fruits; it is wholehearted and straightforward, impartial and unfeigned (free from doubts, wavering, and insincerity)" (James 3:17 AMP).

James speaks here of God's wisdom. In contrast to earthly wisdom or wisdom that comes from demonic forces, God's wisdom is full of mercy, not judgment. Again, the Bible says mercy triumphs over judgment. God's wisdom is no respecter of persons. It doesn't play favorites. God's wisdom brings good fruit.

> "And the harvest of righteousness (of conformity to God's will in thought and deed) is [the fruit of the seed] sown in peace by those who work for and make peace [in themselves and in others, that peace which means concord, agreement, and harmony between individuals, with undisturbedness, in a peaceful mind

free from fears and agitating passions and moral conflicts]" (James 3:17-18 AMP).

God's wisdom leads people to Him, not toward their own soulish desires. God's wisdom breeds unity, not discord. God's wisdom brings healing, not strife. God's wisdom offers comfort, not fear. It's time to get out of the judge's seat.

GET OUT OF THE JUDGE'S SEAT

Prophets who walk in arrogance and pride rather than humility will find it easy to find fault with anything and everything around them. It's a critical spirit and it clogs up your prophetic pipes and good. How can you stand in the gap if you are judgmental, critical and negative?

Prophets who have those traits are more likely to debate over who prophesied a disaster first and e-mail their mailing list with proof positive than to stand in the gap or weep over sin in the land. They may issue calls for intercession, but they are among the first to brag over having pegged the event and seem pleased to have done so. Is their heart really to make up a hedge of protection? Or does pride get in the way?

We cannot sit in judgment over people and cities. This not our place.

> "Brothers, do not slander one another. Anyone who speaks against his brother or judges him speaks against the law and judges it. When you judge the law, you are not keeping it, but sitting in judgment on it. There is only one Lawgiver and Judge, the one who is able to save and destroy. But you—who are you to judge your neighbor?" (James 4:11-12)

Judge not, lest ye be judged (Matthew 7:1). If you have a word of warning about judgment, have enough fear of the Lord to make sure it is really God, and have enough wherewithal to do as Abraham and Moses did: Plead for mercy to stop the tragedy. I'm not saying that God will never pronounce judgment. I can't say that, but He alone can determine this. It's not our place. I do believe this: He'd rather show mercy. God is love (1 John 4:8). Love's first instinct is not to destroy its children.

Although no man can tame the tongue, I believe the Spirit of God can. We will never be perfect so long as we are engaged in this flesh, but we can certainly yield ourselves to the Holy Spirit's unction to speak or not to speak. I challenge you today to seek the Holy Spirit over this issue for yourself. I challenge you to "let all bitterness, and wrath, and anger, and clamour, and evil speaking, be put away from you, with all malice: and be ye kind one to another, tenderhearted, forgiving one another, even as God for Christ's sake hath forgiven you" (Ephesians 4:31-32).

PROPHETIC KEYS

+ If the holy prophets have been speaking about the restitution of all things since the world began, then shouldn't holy prophets still be speaking about the restitution of all things? Restitution is the act of restoring, not the act of destroying.

+ You will prophesy according to your revelation of who Jesus is. And you can't prophesy beyond your knowledge of Him. Since the spirit of prophecy is the testimony of Jesus, according to Revelation 19:10, then it seems clear that your testimony of Jesus will color the spirit of the prophecy you release.

◆ If maturity is the ability to think, speak and act on your feelings within the bounds of dignity, then the measure of maturity is how spiritual you become during the midst of your frustrations.

◆ If you know you are bitter, don't try to deny it. If you know that your prophetic flow is salty instead of sweet, then don't let your pride keep you from admitting it and wind up deceived.

◆ Prophets who walk in arrogance and pride rather than in humility will find it easy to find fault with anything and everything around them. It's a critical spirit and it clogs up your prophetic pipes and good. How can you stand in the gap if you are judgmental, critical and negative?

◆ Although no man can tame the tongue, I believe the Spirit of God can. We will never be perfect so long as we are engaged in this flesh, but we can certainly yield ourselves to the Holy Spirit's unction to speak or not to speak.

Chapter 12

THE
SELF-IMPRISONED
PROPHET

For rebellion is as the sin of witchcraft, and stubbornness is as iniquity and idolatry. Because thou hast rejected the word of the Lord, he hath also rejected thee from being king. (1 Samuel 15:23)

It was 1830. Joseph Smith organized the Church of Jesus Christ of Latter Day Saints, otherwise known as the Mormon church. The United States Congress passed the Indian Removal Act, a law that sent American Indians from the eastern states to the West against the better judgment of Christian missionaries. And George Wilson and James Porter sat in an American prison. Their crime was robbing a U.S. mail carrier and putting his life in jeopardy. Their sentence was death. Their only hope was a presidential pardon.

There sat Wilson and Porter on death row, waiting for the hangman to slip nooses around their necks. After Porter was executed, Wilson's influential friends went straight to President Andrew Jackson and interceded for his life. They pled for mercy – and he heard their cries. Jackson issued a formal pardon that would negate Wilson's death sentence. Rather than rejoicing, though, Wilson refused the pardon. According to the official report, he chose to "waive and decline any advantage or protection which might be supposed to arise from the pardon referred to." Wilson also said he "had nothing to say, and that he did not wish in any manner to avail himself in order to avoid sentence."

The court tried to force the pardon on him, but Wilson continued to refuse. The matter finally made its way all the way up to the Supreme Court, where Chief Justice John Marshall heard the case and wrote the following decision: "A pardon is a slip of paper, the value of which is determined by the acceptance of the person to be pardoned. If it is refused, it is no pardon. George Wilson must be hanged." And so Wilson was hanged, but not because he robbed a mailman. Wilson was hanged because he was too stubborn to accept his way of escape.

IMPRISONED IN A WHALE'S BELLY

Long before Wilson displayed his stubborn rebellion in an American prison, the Prophet Jonah displayed stubborn rebellion from his own makeshift prison: the belly of a whale. Jonah's experience may be a kid's church favorite, but the story of this Old Testament rascal offers serious warnings for New Testament prophets.

You see, some prophetic potholes just cause a flat tire. Spiritual flat tires slow down your progress, but quick repentance brings a Holy Ghost repair that allows you to get right back on the road and continue your journey in God's will. But make no mistake: persistent stubbornness is no small bump in the road. If you don't swerve out of this roadway crater's path you could derail your entire ministry for all eternity. Don't take my word for it. Just read the Book of Jonah and see for yourself how destructive is the sin of stubbornness.

Although it's true the Book of Jonah has many interpretations and even shadows the death and resurrection of Christ, we all know the Word of God offers layers and levels of revelation. From our prophetic pothole perspective, deeper examination demonstrates two spiritual death knells for prophets: self-will (rebellion) and stubbornness (idolatry). We took an in-depth look at the "self-willed syndrome" in an earlier chapter. As you read on, you'll discover Jonah had several rotten roots in his soul, from stubbornness to pride to rebellion to criticalness. But we have our hands full with stubbornness and we'll do well to focus our attention on this one aspect of Jonah's flawed character.

Indeed, the snare of stubbornness threatens to thwart us all because human nature has a tendency to form strong opinions based on a myriad of factors and life experiences that may or may not be truth. I've heard it said there are as many opinions in the world as there are noses. I think that might be true if everyone had more than one nose. The bottom line is you can't yield to the Holy Ghost if you are stubborn because the very definition of stubbornness is to be unreasonably or perversely unyielding. Perverse and unyielding are not acceptable characteristics for God's mouthpieces.

MULISH.
PERTINACIOUS. IMPENITENT.

Before we get into Jonah's stubbornness, let's look at a few other Biblical examples of how God views this snare. See, some folks deem stubbornness as a quality characteristic – so long as they are being stubborn for a worthy cause. The only cause worthy of a stubborn stance is a cause centered on God's will. Perseverance, though, may be a better word in that case. It was Charles Spurgeon who said, "By perseverance the snail reached the ark." We know that it was God's will for the snail to reach the ark, right?

So I like the word perseverance better because stubbornness is consistently portrayed in the Bible – and in many other instances – in a negative context. Here's my point: Mulish, pertinacious prophets can't be pleasing to God and this unyielding stance can be costly. Yes, there is a price to pay in the prophetic, but it's God's price for righteousness – and even perseverance – not the devil's price for ungodly stubbornness.

Take Pharaoh, for example. God made him stubborn and hardened his heart. Despite signs and wonders, Pharaoh refused to let the children of Israel go. (Read the unfolding drama in Exodus 4-14.) One would think the Israelites would have learned a lesson from the hardships Pharaoh's hardness of heart caused him to suffer. Oh, but no. Not long after entering the wilderness, the Israelites demonstrated to Jehovah they had picked up some of the traits of the evil ruler. The Lord called them stubborn and said they had hard hearts because they murmured and complained. Would you like to wander around the wilderness for 40 years? Want to open the door for your spiritual enemies to gain ground in your life? Just hold on to a stubborn attitude, complain and murmur against God, and you'll never enter the Promised Land.

> "But they would not listen to and obey Me or bend their ear [to Me], but followed the counsels and the stubborn promptings of their own evil hearts and minds, and they turned their backs and went in reverse instead of forward" (Jeremiah 7:24 AMP).

Repeatedly throughout Scripture, God said those who are stubborn and won't listen to His voice have "evil hearts." What an indictment! But if the indictment is woeful, the judgment is even more so. The Apostle Paul told the Romans that callous stubbornness and impenitence of heart store wrath and indignation for

Judgment Day, when God will render to every man according to his works (Romans 2:5-6).

Jesus said to whom much is given much is required. Many people want to be prophets without understanding what will be required. First of all, prophets are called by the will of God alone. You can desire to prophesy, but you should not desire to be a prophet if the Lord hasn't called you to that ministry. The ministry of the prophet demands a complete yielding to the Spirit of God. There is no room for stubbornness. God may have chosen to talk through a mule, but even Balaam's donkey yielded itself to God's purpose, despite the beating the old false prophet gave it. We must do the same.

I like what a former public relations student from Kansas State wrote about stubborn donkeys. I believe we can draw some parallels between these animals and stubborn prophets from her artful illustration. Kathryn Hollingsworth writes, "Their braying voices can carry up to two miles. But do they use this talent to promote positive changes in the barnyard? No, instead they bray for other hard-working animals in the kingdom to submit more and more of their grass and hay. Although donkeys can't provide for themselves, they consider themselves superior to other creatures in the animal kingdom. They attribute this superiority to intellect, because they claim to be tolerant of all the other animals in the kingdom."

Can you see it? I've heard it said that if you want to make a stubborn mule obedient, the best way to do it is to blindfold him and lead him across a shaky bridge. I think it's in the prophet's best interest to quickly obey rather than loudly bray. I can speak from experience. It's no fun to be spiritually blinded and trying to cross a shaky bridge. Suffice it to say that it puts the fear of the Lord in you right quick. Of course, I don't know this first hand, but I would imagine it's not too pleasant to be in the belly of a whale, either. So let's look at the rise and fall of Jonah and avoid the prophetic pothole of stubbornness at all costs.

JONAH'S STERLING TRACK RECORD

The Bible begins Jonah's story with God's instruction to go to Nineveh. But Jonah's chronicle begins long before this prophetic directive. Indeed, Jonah was functioning in his gift, advising kings, and showing himself to be knowledgeable in God's written Word before stubbornness derailed him. Jewish historian Flavius Josephus portrays the picture of an accurate prophet who had his nation's best interests at heart despite the rule of a wicked king.

Jonah served during a time of governmental corruption. Jeroboam was king of Israel. Josephus said the king was haughty and treated God harshly by worshipping idols. He also tells us that Jeroboam caused "ten thousand misfortunes to the people of Israel." Jonah appears on the scene in the 15th year of Jeroboam's reign with a prophetic warfare strategy. Jonah told the king he should wage war against the Syrians, conquer them and repossess land that belonged to Israel according to the boundaries that Joshua established. Jonah's words did not fall to the ground, as Josephus records, "So Jeroboam made an expedition against the Syrians, and overran all their country, as Jonah had foretold."

Jonah probably felt pretty good about himself at that point. His ministry was successful – the Holy Ghost even saw fit to make a record of it in 2 Kings – and it led to a major victory for his nation. Jonah had no problem prophesying that the king should take dominion because he agreed with God's mandate. But the fact that Jeroboam had his back to God as he worshiped idols – and the fact that God was gracious enough to give him dominion over the Syrians anyway – should have taught Jonah some lessons: God's ways are higher than our ways. God's judgment is not always swift. God is full of mercy and grace.

Avoiding prophetic potholes demands an understanding of the ways of God's Spirit. It's not enough just to know the Word of God without knowing the ways of God. Throughout the Book of Jonah, we learn that the prophet understands the word of the Lord. He's not confused about what the Lord said or what the Lord wanted. What he missed is the ways of the Lord. That's an important distinction. We need to know the ways of the Spirit, or at least know His ways well enough to obey even when we don't understand.

ARISE! GO TO NINEVEH

Maybe Jonah was still relishing in his prophetic victory, which played a key role in Jeroboam's dominion-seeking campaign when, suddenly, his next assignment came: Go to Nineveh, Israel's enemy, and bring a message of repentance. Uh oh! Remember, Jonah didn't hesitate to deliver prophetic utterances that instructed the king to defeat his enemies because he agreed with the agenda. But when the word of the Lord came unto him with a message he didn't like, his troubled journey began.

"Now the word of the Lord came unto Jonah the son of Amittai, saying, Arise, go to Nineveh, that great city, and cry against it; for their wickedness is come up before me" (Jonah 1:1-2).

The Lord told Jonah to go to Nineveh, the capital of Assyria, and preach against the wickedness of its society. You can't blame Jonah for trying the spirits on that one. After all, Nineveh was known for its endless cruelty and oppression. It was a city of lies, plunder and blood. On the surface, it couldn't have made any sense to Jonah that God would send him there with a message of repentance.

What's more, Jonah didn't want Nineveh to repent. He wanted to see the judgment of God fall on their heads. Instead, it fell on his. There are many lessons in that. Suffice it to say that we should not judge, lest we be judged. Jonah had a judgmental attitude toward Nineveh. He would have probably jumped at the chance to deliver Nahum's message. Instead, he reaped what he sowed, at least until he repented. But I digress…

A PROPHETIC FUGITIVE

When Jonah received the prophetic word from the Lord – "Arise, go to Nineveh" – he was partially obedient to the command. (Partial obedience doesn't cut it with God. He wants your all in everything.) Jonah arose, alright. But he arose and ran in the opposite direction. The Bible tells us he bought a ticket and boarded a ship headed toward Tarshish.

That reminds me of British Admiral Horatio Nelson and the battle of Copenhagen in 1801.[26] The Danish bombarded his forces for several hours before his commander, Sir Hyde Parker, issued a signal ordering him to stop fighting and retreat. When Nelson's men told him about the signal, he insisted upon seeing it for himself. He was a fighter, and despite the buffeting his forces were taking he wasn't ready to call it quits. So he peered through a telescope and told the men he saw no signal. He was being honest. The only problem was he had deliberately held the telescope to the eye he had lost back in 1794. "I have only one eye," he declared. "I have a right to be blind sometimes."

Like Jonah, Nelson was stubborn and, therefore, he was only partially obedient. Jonah, however, didn't partially obey because he was deaf in one ear and couldn't hear the Lord's entire command. He rebelled against the word of the Lord because he wanted Nineveh to experience the wrath of God instead of the mercy of God. Jonah knew that Jehovah would forgive the people if his message brought them to repentance. In other words, he knew the character of God (which includes mercy) but He didn't understand the ways of God (which dictates when He chooses to extend mercy and when He chooses to exercise judgment).

This is where Jonah's woes begin because rebellion is as the sin of witchcraft (1 Samuel 15:23). Prophets who operate in rebellion are in danger of tapping into a spirit of divination and perverting the voice of God. Divination is foretelling the future by occult means and Isaiah Chapter 44 declares that the Lord makes fools of diviners.

Rebellion made a fool out of Jonah, whose actions brought danger to himself and those around him. The Lord even sent a violent storm upon the sea in response to Jonah's disobedience. The Bible tells us that the ship was about to be broken into pieces and the sailors were terrified for their lives. Meanwhile, Jonah was down in the hold of the ship taking a nap.

SUCCUMBING TO
SPIRITUAL WITCHCRAFT

Who could take a nap in the middle of such a violent tempest? Well, Jesus did but that's because He had the peace of God. Jonah couldn't claim that reason. I wonder, is it possible that Jonah's rebellion opened a door for a spirit of witchcraft to attack him? Spiritual witchcraft is the power of Satan. Fatigue, weariness and slumber are some of its manifestations. When witchcraft attacks, its victims may feel tired, oppressed or depressed. (For a good study on spiritual witchcraft, pick up Jonas Clark's book entitled, "Exposing Spiritual Witchcraft."[27])

What could have caused Jonah to remain fast asleep in the midst of such a life-threatening situation? That's exactly what the ship's captain wanted to know. "So the captain went to him and said, 'How can you sleep? Get up and call on your god" (Jonah 1:6 NLV). Knowing full well he was in rebellion, Jonah was nonetheless too stubborn to call upon his God. So the sailors drew lots to find out who was to blame for the misfortune. Once again we see Jonah's self-willed stubbornness manifest as he refuses to admit it was his own rebellion that angered the Lord and put everyone's lives in danger.

Only when the lot fell on him did Jonah ultimately acknowledge his sin. The sailors then asked Jonah what they could do to end the storm and he told them to cast him into the furious sea. Jonah chose to die instead of repenting to God. How stubborn can a prophet be?

A WHALE OF A PRISON

Jonah's woes were about to worsen because stubbornness is as iniquity and idolatry (1 Samuel 15:23). The stubbornness of following self-will instead of God's will is idolatry and puts the prophet in a precarious position. A vital part of the prophetic ministry is to see, hear and say, but Psalms 115 makes it clear that everyone who trusts in idols takes on the characteristics of idols.

"They have mouths, but they cannot speak; They have eyes, but they cannot see; They have ears, but they cannot hear" (Psalm 115:5-6 NASB).

What good is a prophet who can't see, hear or say? About as good as a prophet who is in the belly of a whale. That's just where Jonah ended up when the sailors threw him into the tumultuous sea. I once found myself in the belly of a whale, figuratively speaking. I didn't understand my circumstances. I didn't agree with the decisions that were being made on my behalf. I submitted to the enemy's pressure instead of submitting to God's will and I ended up in a stinking, rotten situation. No, I wasn't swimming in dead fish and darkness like Jonah, but I was in a lonely place drowning in imaginations without enough light to see the truth.

God will use some interesting methods to get through to His prophets. He sent a whale to pick up a prophet to get his attention. I'm grateful God didn't have to go that far with me. Instead, he sent a blind man. I was in the elevator thinking to myself how unfair my situation was, yet asking God to show me if I was somehow wrong. (Of course, I was sure I was right and was only half-heartedly asking to see the truth. But at least I asked! Ultimately, I did want truth.)

Anyway, I was in the elevator pouting when lo and behold the door opened and a blind man walked in. I mean a storybook blind man. He had the dark glasses, the red and white cane with the vibrating tip and everything. He stumbled around a bit to get into the elevator and he never said a word. I had never seen him before and I never saw him again. Though there were no words exchanged, I could hear God speaking clearly. "Uh-oh, I'm completely blind about my situation," I thought. Suffice it to say I repented and got back on track in a hurry and today I can almost laugh about God sending a blind man to teach me a lesson.

It's funny how a tumultuous situation will eventually force even the most stubborn people to call on God. Jonah was no exception. His situation eventually led him to pray. Jonah recognized his rebellion and stubbornness and finally repented, acknowledging that

"Those who pay regard to false, useless, and worthless idols forsake their own [Source of] mercy and loving-kindness" (Jonah 2:8 AMP).

Jonah promised God to pay what he had vowed and the Lord delivered him from the whale's belly on to dry land. Of course, Jonah wound up preaching in Nineveh, the people repented and that made him angry. Despite his experience in the whale's belly, Jonah didn't seem to learn his lesson. The end of the story is left to our imagination, but the Bible makes no record of the Lord using Jonah again.

YOUR SAFETY NET

Jonah's legend illustrates how critical the restoration of apostolic ministry is. Prophets are undoubtedly vital to the end-time Church. Apostles recognize this truth and welcome prophets to work alongside them to build the Church and equip believers for the work of the ministry. Where other ministry offices have been threatened by or misunderstood the prophet's gift, apostles embrace the grace and seek to build a platform for the prophetic voice. That platform, however, is only accessible by stable prophets who are willing to be held accountable for their utterances.

This accountability does not hinder the prophet, but rather acts as a safety net as there is protection in submission. Consider Nehemiah. Nehemiah was a type of apostle who was called to rebuild the walls of Jerusalem. Who was working alongside Nehemiah? The trumpeters (types of prophets). The trumpeters were submitted to Nehemiah's vision to rebuild the wall and his authority to oversee the completion of that vision. The Old Testament apostolic builder, in turn, welcomed prophetic watchmen to warn him if enemies were approaching (Nehemiah 4:18). So the apostle and prophets worked together in a dangerous situation as several hostile forces sought to kill them in order to stop the work. What would have happened to the trumpeters if they had abandoned Nehemiah's apostolic covering to follow self-will instead of God's will? They may have fallen prey to the Arabs, the

Ammonites or the Ashdodites (types of demonic guards) that opposed the building.

Likewise, New Testament prophets who start off walking in God's will but take a detour into rebellion, stubbornness, pride, lust or any other sinful lifestyle, are apt to fall prey to demonic guards that oppose the building of the glorious Church of Jesus Christ. True apostles are spiritual fathers with the prophets' best interests at heart.

Remember what the Apostle Paul said to the church at Corinth:

> "I'm writing as a father to you, my children. I love you and want you to grow up well, not spoiled. There are a lot of people around who can't wait to tell you what you've done wrong, but there aren't many fathers willing to take the time and effort to help you grow up" (1 Corinthians 4:14-15 MSG).

By speaking the truth in love, however uncomfortable it may be to receive, apostolic fathers are helping to protect New Testament prophets from spirits like Jezebel and witchcraft. An apostolic covering and some fatherly correction may have saved Jonah's ministry, but the last we read of him he was sitting in self-pity outside Nineveh wishing he was dead.

EXAMINE YOURSELF

What has God told you to say or do that you don't agree with? Where is your Nineveh? What is the message you don't want to deliver? What do you think isn't fair? Look, there comes a time in every prophet's walk when he or she has to face some issues like Jonah did. The storyline may not be as dramatic, but the stubborn attitude can certainly stir up plenty of theatrics. Unless you like tragedies, get on God's side. Put your will under His will and seek to understand His ways when you don't understand anything else. Be like Habakkuk instead of Jonah.

See, Jonah was not the only prophet who was confused by God's ways. Habakkuk also had an issue with evil that went unpunished. But we can learn the right way to wade through those types of situations by Habakkuk's response. Let's listen in to his complaint to God in The Message translation. I think this rendition sounds more like today's prophets so you can better relate to his woes.

"God, how long do I have to cry out for help before you listen? How many times do I have to yell, 'Help! Murder! Police!' before you come to the rescue? Why do you force me to look at evil, stare trouble in the face day after day? Anarchy and violence break out, quarrels and fights all over the place. Law and order fall to pieces. Justice is a joke. The wicked have the righteous hamstrung and stand justice on its head" (Habakkuk 1:1-4).

Habakkuk was clearly distraught at the injustices he saw round and about him. He was focused on the circumstances. And he probably didn't like God's response:

"Brace yourself for a shock. Something's about to take place and you're going to find it hard to believe. I'm about to raise up Babylonians to punish you..." (Habakkuk 1:5).

I'm sure the word of the Lord didn't sit well with Habakkuk on first hearing. Would God really use a people more sinful than Israel to punish His chosen people? That didn't make any sense to him. Like Jonah, he didn't understand the ways of God. Unlike Jonah,

Habakkuk's response was to pray instead of pout. Remember, Jonah was too stubborn to pray in the midst of his storm. Habakkuk reminded God of His mercy and splendor and mighty hand of deliverance. By the end of Habakkuk's prayer, he had a new perspective on the ways of God. He understood that God's ways were higher than his ways. He understood that the just shall live by faith. Even though Doomsday awaited at the hand of the Babylonians, Habakkuk made a choice to sing a joyful praise to God and turn cartwheels of joy to his Savior, counting on God's rule to prevail. That attitude gave Habakkuk strength.

AVOIDING THE BIG FISH

Decide today to root out every trace of stubbornness from your soul. Yield completely to the Spirit of God, no matter what He may tell you to do. Avoiding the snare of obstinance is simple: obey the voice of the Lord. Sometimes, God is merely testing our wills to see if we will do what He asks. Once we agree, He will often let us off the hook. That's what happened with Abraham when God told him to sacrifice his son Isaac. Abraham could have stubbornly refused to obey God's voice, but his heart was so pure toward God that he trusted Him even with his most precious possession. Just think. If Abraham had displayed an evil heart and mind that refused to obey the Lord, he may have remained the father of Isaac but he may not have become the father of many nations. Stubbornness is a destiny killer. Avoid it like the plague and yield to the Holy Ghost so you can reach your prophetic destination.

PROPHETIC KEYS

* Jonah's experience may be a kid's church favorite, but the story of this Old Testament rascal offers serious warnings for New Testament prophets.

* Indeed, the snare of stubbornness threatens to thwart us all because human nature has a tendency to form strong opinions based on a myriad of factors and life experiences that may or may not be truth.

* Avoiding prophetic potholes demands an understanding of the ways of God's Spirit. It's not enough just to know the Word of God without knowing the ways of God.

✦   Prophets who operate in rebellion are in danger of tapping into a spirit of divination and perverting the voice of God. Divination is foretelling the future by occult means and Isaiah Chapter 44 declares that the Lord makes fools of diviners.

✦   By speaking the truth in love, however uncomfortable it may be to receive, apostolic fathers are helping to protect New Testament prophets from spirits like Jezebel and witchcraft.

✦   Decide today to root out every trace of stubbornness from your soul. Yield completely to the Spirit of God, no matter what He may tell you to do. Avoiding the snare of obstinane is simple: obey the voice of the Lord.

Afterword

CREATE IN ME
A CLEAN HEART

The Old Testament is full of the stories of great heroes and great failures – and sometimes the same person filled both shoes. We are no different today. We all make mistakes. Some are just bigger and more visible than others. Thank God for His grace and mercy that restores us when we turn to the right or the left of His will. I suppose you could sum up the entire book this way: the heart of the prophetic requires a fear of the Lord.

I believe we need to pray for a fear of the Lord to come upon us. I believe we need to pray for a spirit of wisdom and revelation in the knowledge of Jesus, the eyes of our understanding being enlightened that we may know the hope of His calling (Ephesians 1:17-19). I believe we need to pray that we may live a life worthy of the Lord and may please Him in every way: bearing fruit in every good work, growing in the knowledge of God (Colossians 1:10).

If we really understood the magnitude of wearing the prophetic mantle, we would spend much more time on our face than on our platforms. There is a need for brokenness in the prophetic ministry as the Lord looks for those with clean hearts that can receive, bear and transmit His truth. It takes a clean heart to deliver a pure word. If the word of the Lord settles into a heart full of malice, greed or control, then it may well be profaned.

Exposing spirits and character flaws that open up the door to deception was one of the aims of this book. In doing so, we can reach our goal to flow more accurately in the prophetic and prepare the way for the Lord. I hope this book stirred your heart to fulfill the prophetic call of God on your life and to keep your heart clean. My heart's desire is to see the glorious Church without spot or wrinkle come into manifestation. That's going to require saints who are equipped for the work of ministry. That is going to require apostles, evangelists, pastors, teachers – and prophets – who are determined to stand up for truth. It may get darker in the days ahead. It may get more difficult to stand in the office of the prophet. If our heartbeat is one with God's, then we will be thrilled to hear him say,

> "Well done thou good and faithful servant" (Matthew 25:23).

We need to cry out for clean hearts, for the heart of the prophetic is a clean one. Forgive yourself. Forgive those who have wronged you. Forgive God if you feel you need to (though God does nothing that needs to be forgiven). Walk in love, so that all men might know that you are Christ's disciples. We can pray David's petition right now, the cry for mercy after the Prophet Nathan exposed his sin. We find this beautiful prayer in Psalm 51 of the New International Version of the Bible:

> Have mercy on me, O God, according to your unfailing love; according to your great compassion blot out my transgressions. Wash away all my iniquity and cleanse me from my sin. For I know my transgressions, and my sin is always before me. Against you, you only, have I sinned and done what is evil in your sight, so that you are proved right when you speak and justified when you judge.

Surely I was sinful at birth, sinful from the time my mother conceived me. Surely you desire truth in the inner parts; you teach me wisdom in the inmost place. Cleanse me with hyssop, and I will be clean; wash me, and I will be whiter than snow. Let me hear joy and gladness; let the bones you have crushed rejoice. Hide your face from my sins and blot out all my iniquity.

Create in me a pure heart, O God, and renew a steadfast spirit within me. Do not cast me from your presence or take your Holy Spirit from me. Restore to me the joy of your salvation and grant me a willing spirit, to sustain me. Then I will teach transgressors your ways, and sinners will turn back to you. Save me from bloodguilt, O God, the God who saves me, and my tongue will sing of your righteousness.

O Lord, open my lips, and my mouth will declare your praise. You do not delight in sacrifice, or I would bring it; you do not take pleasure in burnt offerings. The sacrifices of God are a broken spirit; a broken and contrite heart, O God, you will not despise. In your good pleasure make Zion prosper; build up the walls of Jerusalem. Then there will be righteous sacrifices, whole burnt offerings to delight you; then bulls will be offered on your altar.

Amen and amen.

I'll admit, it can be discouraging at times to see some put a blight on prophetic ministry with their merchandising, judgments and curses. Truthfully, I cringe every time I read about merchandisers rolling through town under the guise of a revival to drain the coffers of the region's local church members. And I feel downright nauseous when I watch prophets claim credit for predicting a natural disaster and calling it the wrath of God. I know you do, too.

Despite it all, though, I remain encouraged. There is a bright future for prophetic ministry. The Lord has opened my eyes, and I pray that He will open yours. What do I see? Well, I see that spirits of divination, religion, witchcraft, Jezebel, religion, Baal and their wicked cohorts are waging war against prophetic ministry, to discredit it and delay the glorious Church. But, more importantly, I also see this: they that be with us are more than they that be with them (2 Kings 6:16). I see horses and chariots of fire round about the Melchizedek prophets. I see prophets turning hearts, preparing the way, reforming, standing in the gap, making up the hedge – fulfilling their destinies and leaving legacies. I see you being all God has called you to be.

Hallelujah! Let the prophets arise and go forth with clean hearts in the spirit of Elijah!

Footnotes

1. *The Elijah Task: A Call to Prophets and Intercessors.* John and Paula Sandford

2. *100 Best After-Dinner Stories.* Phyllis Schindler

3. *Extreme Prophetic Studies.* Jonas Clark

4. *Miriam-Webster's Dictionary.* www.m-w.com

5. *Global Language Monitor.* www.languagemonitor.com

6. *Prophetic Ministry: A Classic Study on the Nature of a Prophet.* T. Austin Sparks

7. *30 Pieces of Silver.* Jonas Clark

8. *Miriam-Webster's Dictionary.* www.m-w.com

9. *Miriam-Webster's Dictionary.* www.m-w.com

10. *Purifying the Prophetic: Breaking Free from the Spirit of Self-Fulfillment.* R. Loren Sandford

11. *Jezebel: Seducing Goddess of War.* Jonas Clark

12. *Life After Rejection.* Jonas Clark.

13. *Miriam-Webster's Dictionary.* www.m-w.com

14. *Prophetic Operations.* Jonas Clark

15. *Miriam-Webster's Dictionary.* www.m-w.com

16. *Miriam-Webster's Dictionary.* www.m-w.com

17. *Japan Today.* www.japantoday.com/jp/news/355037

18. *ExChristian.net* exchristian.net/2/2005/09/farrakhan-god-punishing-us-for-iraq.php

19. *ABC News.* abcnews.go.com/International/wireStory?id=3168489

20. *CBS News.* www.cbsnews.com/stories/2006/04/04/national/main1467778.shtml

21. *The ABC News.* www.abc.net.au/news/stories/2003/12/08/1005971.htm

22. *Blog Critics* blogcritics.org/archives/2005/02/09/174705.php

23. *The Prophetic Ministry.* Rick Joyner

24. *Miriam-Webster's Dictionary.* www.m-w.com

25. *Developing Your Prophetic Gifting.* Graham Cooke

26. Anecdotage.com.

27. *Exposing Spiritual Witchcraft.* Jonas Clark

ABOUT THE AUTHOR

Jennifer LeClaire is a prophetic voice and teacher whose passion is to see the lost come to Christ and equip believers to understand the will and ways of God. She carries a reforming voice that seeks to turn hearts to the Lord and edify the Body of Christ.

Jennifer has a powerful testimony of God's power to set the captives free and claim beauty for ashes. She shares her story with women who need to understand the love and grace of God in a lost and dying world.

Jennifer was the founding editor of The Voice magazine, and remains a frequent contributor to major international Christian magazines and publications. Some of her work is archived in the Flower Pentecostal Heritage Museum.

Jennifer is a community chaplain for South Florida Jail Ministries, a non-profit ministry that seeks to restore individuals and families to psychological, social, physical and spiritual health.

Jennifer is a prolific author who has written several books, including "The Heart of the Prophetic," "A Prophet's Heart," "Doubtless: Faith that Overcomes the World" and "The Seven Habits of Highly Effective Christian Living." Her materials have been translated into Spanish and Korean.

Hungry for more? Visit JenniferLeClaire.org to find more of Jennifer's books, teaching CDs, podcasts, artices, videos and more, incuding:

A Prophet's Heart: Avoiding the Doorway to Deception

Doubtless: Faith that Overcomes the World

Fervent Faith: Discover how a fervent spirit is a defense against the devil

You can also visit Jennifer online on:

http://www.facebook.com/propheticbooks

http://www.myspace.com/propheticbooks

http://www.youtube.com/jnleclaire

http://www.twitter.com/propheticbooks

CPSIA information can be obtained at www.ICGtesting.com
Printed in the USA
LVOW07s1554120916

504264LV00001B/39/P